GLOBAL WARMING

OPPOSING VIEWPOINTS ®

Cynthia A. Bily, *Book Editor*

Bonnie Szumski, *Publisher*
Helen Cothran, *Managing Editor*

OPPOSING
VIEWPOINTS®
SERIES

GREENHAVEN PRESS

An imprint of Thomson Gale, a part of The Thomson Corporation

THOMSON

GALE

Detroit • New York • San Francisco • San Diego • New Haven, Conn.
Waterville, Maine • London • Munich

THOMSON

GALE

LIBRARY OF CONGRESS CATALOGING-IN-PUBLICATION DATA

Global warming / Cynthia A. Bily, book editor.
   p. cm. — (Opposing viewpoints series)
Includes bibliographical references and index.
ISBN 0-7377-2935-X (lib. : alk. paper) — ISBN 0-7377-2936-8 (pbk. : alk. paper)
   1. Global warming. I. Bily, Cynthia A. II. Series: Opposing viewpoints series
(Unnumbered)
QC981.8.G56G574 2006
363.738'74—dc22
                                        2005052779

Printed in the United States of America

> "Congress shall make no law. . . abridging the freedom of speech, or of the press."

First Amendment to the U.S. Constitution

The basic foundation of our democracy is the First Amendment guarantee of freedom of expression. The Opposing Viewpoints Series is dedicated to the concept of this basic freedom and the idea that it is more important to practice it than to enshrine it.

Contents

Why Consider Opposing Viewpoints?

"The only way in which a human being can make some approach to knowing the whole of a subject is by hearing what can be said about it by persons of every variety of opinion and studying all modes in which it can be looked at by every character of mind. No wise man ever acquired his wisdom in any mode but this."

John Stuart Mill

In our media-intensive culture it is not difficult to find differing opinions. Thousands of newspapers and magazines and dozens of radio and television talk shows resound with differing points of view. The difficulty lies in deciding which opinion to agree with and which "experts" seem the most credible. The more inundated we become with differing opinions and claims, the more essential it is to hone critical reading and thinking skills to evaluate these ideas. Opposing Viewpoints books address this problem directly by presenting stimulating debates that can be used to enhance and teach these skills. The varied opinions contained in each book examine many different aspects of a single issue. While examining these conveniently edited opposing views, readers can develop critical thinking skills such as the ability to compare and contrast authors' credibility, facts, argumentation styles, use of persuasive techniques, and other stylistic tools. In short, the Opposing Viewpoints Series is an ideal way to attain the higher-level thinking and reading skills so essential in a culture of diverse and contradictory opinions.

In addition to providing a tool for critical thinking, Opposing Viewpoints books challenge readers to question their own strongly held opinions and assumptions. Most people form their opinions on the basis of upbringing, peer pressure, and personal, cultural, or professional bias. By reading carefully balanced opposing views, readers must directly confront new ideas as well as the opinions of those with whom they disagree. This is not to simplistically argue that everyone who reads opposing views will—or should—change his or her opinion. Instead, the series enhances readers' understanding of their own views by encouraging confrontation with opposing ideas. Careful examination of others' views can lead to the readers' understanding of the logical inconsistencies in their own opinions, perspective on why they hold an opinion, and the consideration of the possibility that their opinion requires further evaluation.

Evaluating Other Opinions

To ensure that this type of examination occurs, Opposing Viewpoints books present all types of opinions. Prominent spokespeople on different sides of each issue as well as well-known professionals from many disciplines challenge the reader. An additional goal of the series is to provide a forum for other, less known, or even unpopular viewpoints. The opinion of an ordinary person who has had to make the decision to cut off life support from a terminally ill relative, for example, may be just as valuable and provide just as much insight as a medical ethicist's professional opinion. The editors have two additional purposes in including these less known views. One, the editors encourage readers to respect others' opinions—even when not enhanced by professional credibility. It is only by reading or listening to and objectively evaluating others' ideas that one can determine whether they are worthy of consideration. Two, the inclusion of such viewpoints encourages the important critical thinking skill of objectively evaluating an author's credentials and bias. This evaluation will illuminate an author's reasons for taking a particular stance on an issue and will aid in readers' evaluation of the author's ideas.

It is our hope that these books will give readers a deeper understanding of the issues debated and an appreciation of the complexity of even seemingly simple issues when good and honest people disagree. This awareness is particularly important in a democratic society such as ours in which people enter into public debate to determine the common good. Those with whom one disagrees should not be regarded as enemies but rather as people whose views deserve careful examination and may shed light on one's own.

Thomas Jefferson once said that "difference of opinion leads to inquiry, and inquiry to truth." Jefferson, a broadly educated man, argued that "if a nation expects to be ignorant and free . . . it expects what never was and never will be." As individuals and as a nation, it is imperative that we consider the opinions of others and examine them with skill and discernment. The Opposing Viewpoints Series is intended to help readers achieve this goal.

David L. Bender and Bruno Leone,
Founders

Introduction

"As new conditions and problems arise beyond the power of men and women to meet as individuals, it becomes the duty of the Government itself to find new remedies with which to meet them."

—*Franklin Delano Roosevelt,*
Public Papers and Addresses

When leaders from the Group of Eight (G-8) industrialized nations met in Scotland in the summer of 2005, British prime minister Tony Blair, the host of the summit, put global warming at the top of the agenda. Seven of the eight nations—Great Britain, Canada, France, Germany, Italy, Japan, and Russia—had already ratified the Kyoto Protocol, an international treaty calling on nations to reduce their greenhouse gas emissions. Of the G-8 nations, only the United States, the world's largest producer of greenhouse gas emissions, had rejected the treaty. Hoping he could encourage the United States to agree on specific targets for reducing emissions, Blair invited leaders of China, India, and other developing nations to join the discussion.

U.S. president George W. Bush, however, held firm and did not agree to reduce U.S. emissions to pre-1990 levels. In holding to his position, he disappointed many people in Europe and Asia but pleased many in the United States. Bush accepted the criticism that other nations leveled at him because he believed he was acting in the best interests of his own people. He continued to argue that the treaty was not an effective way to address climate change, and he announced at the end of the summit, "I fully recognize that by making that point, it was not a popular position in parts of the world. Now is the time to get beyond the Kyoto period and develop a strategy forward."

American opposition to the Kyoto Protocol has been consistent since 2001, when Bush first announced that the United States would not sign the treaty. One problem with Kyoto, in many Americans' eyes, is that it does not demand that developing nations reduce their greenhouse gas emissions. It seemed fairer to those who signed the treaty to ask nations like the United States and Canada, who consume large amounts of energy for luxuries, to cut back their consumption, rather than to ask poorer nations to reduce theirs. Energy is consumed in these countries for what many consider the essentials of modern life, such as refrigeration. However, the United States has argued that it is unfair to ask it to make sacrifices that others are not being asked to make.

Bush was certainly correct when saying that reducing emissions would require sacrifices. Most of the suggestions for addressing global warming call for large-scale changes, such as revolutionizing the way electricity is produced, or regulating what kinds of cars and appliances can be made and sold, or limiting the amount of emissions a company or a city could produce. The American economy depends heavily on the manufacturing of cars, appliances, and other energy-consuming machines, and on producing enough power to keep the factories and these products running. Making sweeping changes in energy production and consumption would affect consumers and workers alike. Declaring his refusal to sign the treaty, Bush stated, "For America, complying with those mandates would have a negative economic impact, with layoffs of workers and price increases for consumers. And when you evaluate all these flaws, most reasonable people will understand that it's not sound public policy."

No one knows for sure how reducing emissions would affect the United States. Certainly, jobs would be lost in manufacturing and transportation, but new jobs might be created in producing alternative energy sources and new kinds of energy-saving products. The Pew Center on Global Climate Change claims that "Kyoto will produce economic benefits rather than costs, by inducing innovation and giving industry in Europe and Japan a head start in developing new technologies to cut emissions." Prices would rise for many products, but people might learn to enjoy having less. What is undeniable is that the changes would be drastic. Analyst Donn Dears describes what might happen if the nation reduced its greenhouse emissions by almost a third: "Visualize the following: A 30% reduction in all power generation other than nuclear, hydro or renewables. A 30% reduction in

11

the number of miles driven by families using their cars. A 30% reduction in the number of miles driven by commercial trucks. A 30% reduction in the use of farm vehicles. A 30% reduction in the number of airline flights. A 30% reduction in manufacturing, ranching, refining and chemical processes emitting greenhouse gases." Before Bush could commit the United States to a program like this, he would need to be very confident that it would be for the best.

Even those who would like to see the United States and other countries severely reduce their greenhouse gas emissions acknowledge that the costs would be dramatic. Foreign policy analyst Tom Athansiou, for example, considers what would happen if every person on the planet were allotted the same amount of energy consumption and carbon emission: "To get to sustainable levels, the average citizen of the U.S. would have to cut his or her emissions by over 90%." Writer Bill McKibben agrees: "To reduce the amount of CO_2 pouring into the atmosphere means dramatically reducing the amount of fossil fuel being consumed. Which means changing the underpinning of the planet's entire economy and altering our most ingrained personal habits. Even under the best scenarios, this will involve something more like a revolution than a technical fix."

Another challenge before the president and Congress is that they were elected to serve the interests of their constituents. The American people have not yet asked the federal government to restrict their use of cars and air conditioners. In fact, in the years since global warming was first raised as a possible problem, the United States has *increased* its energy consumption and greenhouse gas emissions every year, as cars have gotten bigger, air conditioners and other appliances have gotten cheaper, and the population and the economy of the United States have grown. If Congress and the president were to enact strict reductions in greenhouse gas emissions, they would have to do so over the objections of many of their constituents.

In deciding what approach to take on climate change, the United States must decide whether its primary responsibility is to protect the jobs and the well-being of U.S. citizens even if it might hurt people in other countries, or to help protect the planet even if it might lower the standard of living of many Americans. The government also must balance the needs and wishes of those who are alive today (and who vote today) against the needs and wishes of unborn generations, who will be affected by any climate change that occurs. Most elected officials have decided to take more time to study the issue before they take action. They do not want to risk imposing restrictions that could turn out to be unnecessary.

To be sure, America's rejection of the Kyoto Treaty does not mean the discussion is over. In June 2005 the U.S. Senate passed a "Sense of the Senate" resolution, recognizing for the first time that global warming is happening, that it is caused by human activities, and that mandatory steps should be taken to address the problem. Fred Krupp, president of Environmental Defense, called the resolution "a clear shift in climate policy" in that "the Senate is clearly moving beyond a discussion of whether America will begin to deal with the issue, and instead is beginning to focus on what to do about it." Still, the resolution passed only by a vote of 53 to 44. Nearly half of the senators do not believe that the dangers of climate change outweigh the risks to their constituents' way of life.

The position of the U.S. government is difficult, indeed. In trying to strike a balance between the needs of the global community and its own citizens, it risks the censure of both. However, a consensus has developed that the federal government must act on climate change. Problems of such huge scope can only be solved by nations, not by individuals, many experts claim. Although one person might decide to ride a bicycle instead of driving a car, the earth's atmosphere is too large to be affected measurably by this simple change, they point out. Vice President Dick Cheney explains that "conservation may be a sign of personal virtue, but it is not a sufficient basis for a sound, comprehensive national energy policy."

The Kyoto Protocol will expire in 2010, when nations must again meet and attempt to establish a new international policy for addressing global warming. The United States government will be expected to play an important role in those discussions. In the meantime, America's leaders seem destined to move slowly on climate change, continuing to study the economic, social, and political impacts of global warming and the proposed actions to address it. The authors in *Opposing Viewpoints: Global Warming* present a range of answers to four central questions: Is the threat of global warming real? What causes global warming? What will be the effects of global warming? Should measures be taken to combat global warming? U.S. policy makers will be examining these questions as they plan ways to address climate change. As President Bush states, "We want to know more about [global warming]. It's easier to solve a problem when you know a lot about it."

CHAPTER 1

Is the Threat of Global Warming Real?

Chapter Preface

Like any scientific theory, global warming has those who believe it to be a fact, those who believe it is a possibility, and those who do not believe it at all. Many scientists have concluded that the average temperature of the Earth has risen over the past hundred and fifty years, and that this rise is due to human influences. They warn that this climate change will lead to serious consequences, including a rise in sea level, changes in water availability, and extreme weather events unless the human actions that have caused it are stopped. Other scientists have looked at the same data and seen no evidence of global warming. They contend that the Earth's average temperatures are not changing, and that those who think they have proof of climate change are what Citizens for a Sound Economy call "radical fringe environmentalists" or "extremists," seeing only what they expect to see.

Nonscientists may find it difficult to understand how there can be such a wide difference of opinion. Science is supposed to be based on facts—things that can be proven true or false. Either global warming is happening or it is not, and laypeople sometimes assume that science can determine the answer. But science is in many ways a gathering of questions, not of answers; it involves testing and retesting ideas with an open and curious mind. Predictions of global warming are derived from observations, from computer models, and from well-reasoned guesses about what is statistically probable. *New Yorker* reporter Elizabeth Kolbert points out that "even the most detailed climate models can only approximate reality very crudely, and it's hard to know in advance which will prove to be the most accurate."

The problem, of course, is that only time will tell. If environmentalists are right in saying the need for action is urgent, by the time it is proven that global warming is causing serious harm, it may be too late to stop it. If the skeptics are right and there is no human-made global warming, by the time it is proven that global warming is *not* a threat, societies will have wasted billions of dollars chasing a solution to an imagined problem—dollars that scientist Sallie Baliunas points out could have been spent to meet "major environmental, health, and welfare challenges." The stakes are high, indeed.

In the following chapter scientists, journalists, and other researchers consider the evidence that has been presented to support the theory of global warming, and ask whether the conclusions drawn from it are based on sound science. The debate in this chapter comes down to the central question about global warming: Is it real?

*"Dangerous climate change is taking place,
and . . . time is running out."*

Global Warming Poses a Serious Threat

Geoffrey Lean

In early 2005 British prime minister Tony Blair gathered two hundred scientists to advise him about the dangers posed by global warming. In the following viewpoint Geoffrey Lean summarizes the scientists' presentations, reporting that global warming will lead to natural disasters, animal extinction, disease, and starvation. Technology is available to alleviate much of the impending disaster, Lean writes, but he warns that governments must act soon to address the problem before it is too late. Lean is environmental editor of the British newspaper the *Independent*, and coauthor of *Atlas of the Environment*.

As you read, consider the following questions:

1. According to the author, why did Prime Minister Tony Blair want to learn more about global climate change?
2. How does warmer water affect bird populations, as explained by Lean?
3. According to Lean, how could global warming make northern Europe colder?

Future historians, looking back from a much hotter and less hospitable world, are likely to pay special attention to the first few weeks of 2005. As they puzzle over how a whole generation could have sleepwalked into distaster—destroying the climate that has allowed human civilization to flourish over the past 11,000 years—they may well identify [these] weeks as the time when the last alarms sounded.

[In February 2005,] 200 of the world's leading climate scientists—meeting at [British prime minister] Tony Blair's request at the [National Meteorological] Office's new headquarters [the Met] at Exeter—issued the most urgent warning to date that dangerous climate change is taking place, and that time is running out.

[In mid-February] the Kyoto Protocol, the international treaty that tries to control global warming, [went] into force after a seven-year delay. But it is clear that the protocol does not go nearly far enough.

The alarms have been going off since the beginning of one of the warmest Januaries on record. First, Dr Rajendra Pachauri—chairman of the official Intergovernmental Panel on Climate Change (IPCC)—told a UN conference in Mauritius that the pollution which causes global warming has reached "dangerous" levels.

Then the biggest-ever study of climate change, based at Oxford University, reported that it could prove to be twice as catastrophic as the IPCC's worst predictions. And an international task force—also reporting to Tony Blair, and co-chaired by his close ally, Stephen Byers—concluded that we could reach "the point of no return" in a decade.

Finally, the [United Kingdom] head of Shell [Oil], Lord Oxburgh, took time out—just before his company reported record profits mainly achieved by selling oil, one of the main causes of the problem—to warn that unless governments take urgent action there "will be a disaster".

A Conference on Climate

But it was . . . at the Met Office's futuristic glass headquarters, incongruously set in a dreary industrial estate on the outskirts of Exeter, that it all came together. The conference had been called by the Prime Minister to advise him on how to "avoid dangerous climate change". He needed help in persuading the world to prioritize the issue this year during Britain's presidencies of the EU [European Union] and the G8 group of economic powers.

The conference opened with the Secretary of State for the Environment, Margaret Beckett, warning that "a significant impact" from global warming "is already inevitable". It continued with presentations from top scientists and economists from every continent. These showed that some dangerous climate change was already taking place and that catastrophic events once thought highly improbable were now seen as likely. Avoiding the worst was technically simple and economically cheap, they said, provided that governments could be persuaded to take immediate action.

Sack. Copyright © 2004 by Cowles Media Co. Reproduced by permission of Knight Ridder/Tribune Information.

About halfway through I realized that I had been here before. In the summer of 1986 the world's leading nuclear experts gathered in Vienna for an inquest into the [nuclear reactor] accident at Chernobyl. The head of the Russian delegation showed a film shot from a helicopter, and we suddenly found ourselves gazing down on the red-hot exposed reactor core.

It was all, of course, much less dramatic at Exeter. But as paper followed learned paper, once again a group of world authorities were staring at a crisis they had devoted their lives to trying to avoid.

I am willing to bet there were few in the room who did not sense their children or grandchildren standing invisibly at their shoulders. The conference formally concluded that climate change was "already occurring" and that "in many cases the risks are more serious than previously thought". But the cautious scientific language scarcely does justice to the sense of the meeting.

Catastrophe Looms

We learned that glaciers are shrinking around the world. Arctic sea ice has lost almost half its thickness in recent decades. Natural disasters are increasing rapidly around the world. Those caused by the weather—such as droughts, storms, and floods—are rising three times faster than those—such as earthquakes—that are not.

We learned that bird populations in the North Sea collapsed last year [2004], after the sand eels on which they feed left its warmer waters—and how the number of scientific papers recording changes in ecosystems due to global warming has escalated from 14 to more than a thousand in five years.

Worse, leading scientists warned of catastrophic changes that once they had dismissed as "improbable". The meeting was particularly alarmed by powerful evidence, first reported in [British newspaper] *The Independent on Sunday* last July [2004], that the oceans are slowly turning acid, threatening all marine life.

Professor Chris Rapley, director of the British Antarctic Survey, presented new evidence that the West Antarctic ice sheet is beginning to melt, threatening eventually to raise sea levels by 15ft: 90 per cent of the world's people live near current sea levels. Recalling that the IPCC's last report had called Antarctica "a slumbering giant", he said: "I would say that this is now an awakened giant".

Professor Mike Schlesinger, of the University of Illinois,

reported that the shutdown of the Gulf Stream, once seen as a "low probability event", was now 45 per cent likely this century, and 70 per cent probable by 2200. If it comes sooner rather than later it will be catastrophic for Britain and northern Europe, giving us a climate like Labrador (which shares our latitude) even as the rest of the world heats up: if it comes later it could be beneficial, moderating the worst of the warming.

A Consensus Emerges

The experts at Exeter were virtually unanimous about the danger, mirroring the attitude of the climate science community as a whole: humanity is to blame. There were a few skeptics at Exeter, including Andrei Illarionov, an adviser to Russia's President [Vladimir] Putin, who last year called the Kyoto Protocol "an interstate Auschwitz". But in truth it is much easier to find skeptics among media pundits in London or neo-cons in Washington than among climate scientists. Even the few contrarian climatologists publish little research to support their views, concentrating on questioning the work of others.

Now a new scientific consensus is emerging—that the warming must be kept below an average increase of two degrees centigrade if catastrophe is to be avoided. This almost certainly involves keeping concentrations of carbon dioxide, the main cause of climate change, below 400 parts per million.

Unfortunately we are almost there, with concentrations exceeding 370ppm and rising, but experts at the conference concluded that we could go briefly above the danger level so long as we brought it down rapidly afterwards. They added that this would involve the world reducing emissions by 50 per cent by 2050—and rich countries cutting theirs by 30 per cent by 2020.

Economists stressed there is little time for delay. If action is put off for a decade, it will need to be twice as radical; if it has to wait 20 years, it will cost between three and seven times as much.

The good news is that it can be done with existing technology, by cutting energy waste, expanding the use of renewable sources, growing trees and crops (which remove carbon dioxide from the air) to turn into fuel, capturing the gas before it is released from power stations, and—maybe—using more nuclear energy.

The better news is that it would not cost much: one estimate suggested the cost would be about 1 per cent of Europe's GNP [Gross National Product] spread over 20 years; another suggested it meant postponing an expected fivefold increase in world wealth by just two years. Many experts believe combating global warming would increase prosperity, by bringing in new technologies.

The big question is whether governments will act. President [George W.] Bush's opposition to international action remains the greatest obstacle. Tony Blair, by almost universal agreement, remains the leader with the best chance of persuading him to change his mind.

But so far the Prime Minister has been more influenced by the President than the other way round. He appears to be moving away from fighting for the pollution reductions needed in favor of agreeing on a vague pledge to bring in new technologies sometime in the future.

By then it will be too late. And our children and grandchildren will wonder—as we do in surveying, for example, the drift into the First World War—"how on earth could they be so blind?"

Water Wars

What could happen? Wars break out over diminishing water resources as populations grow and rains fail.

How would this come about? Over 25 per cent more people than at present are expected to live in countries where water is scarce in the future, and global warming will make it worse.

How likely is it? Former UN [United Nations] chief Boutros Boutros-Ghali has long said that the next Middle East war will be fought for water, not oil.

Disappearing Nations

What could happen? Low-lying islands such as the Maldives and Tuvalu—with highest points only a few feet above sea-level—will disappear off the face of the Earth.

How would this come about? As the world heats up, sea levels are rising, partly because glaciers are melting, and partly because the water in the oceans expands as it gets warmer.

How likely is it? Inevitable. Even if global warming stopped today, the seas would continue to rise for centuries. Some small islands have already sunk forever. A year ago, Tuvalu was briefly submerged.

Flooding

What could happen? London, New York, Tokyo, Bombay, many other cities and vast areas of countries from Britain to Bangladesh disappear under tens of feet of water, as the seas rise dramatically.

How would this come about? Ice caps in Greenland and Antarctica melt. The Greenland ice sheet would raise sea levels by more than 20ft, the West Antarctic ice sheet by another 15ft.

How likely is it? Scientists used to think it unlikely, but this year reported that the melting of both ice caps had begun. It will take hundreds of years, however, for the seas to rise that much.

Uninhabitable Earth

What could happen? Global warming escalates to the point where the world's whole climate abruptly switches, turning it permanently into a much hotter and less hospitable planet.

How would this come about? A process involving "positive feedback" causes the warming to fuel itself, until it reaches a point that finally tips the climate pattern over.

How likely is it? Abrupt flips have happened in the prehistoric past. Scientists believe this is unlikely, at least in the foreseeable future, but increasingly they are refusing to rule it out.

Rainforest Fires

What could happen? Famously wet tropical forests, such as those in the Amazon, go up in flames, destroying the world's richest wildlife habitats and releasing vast amounts of carbon dioxide to speed global warming.

How would this come about? Britain's Met Office predicted in 1999 that much of the Amazon will dry out and die within 50 years, making it ready for sparks—from humans or lightning—to set it ablaze.

How likely is it? Very, if the predictions turn out to be right. Already there have been massive forest fires in Borneo and Amazonia, casting palls of highly polluting smoke over vast areas.

The Big Freeze

What could happen? Britain and northern Europe get much colder because the Gulf Stream, which provides as much heat as the sun in winter, fails.

How would this come about? Melting polar ice sends fresh water into the North Atlantic. The less salty water fails to generate the underwater current which the Gulf Stream needs.

How likely is it? About even for a Gulf Stream failure this century, said scientists last week.

Starvation

What could happen? Food production collapses in Africa, for example, as rainfall dries up and droughts increase. As farmland turns to desert, people flee in the millions in search of food.

How would this come about? Rainfall is expected to decrease by up to 60 per cent in winter and 30 per cent in summer in southern Africa this century. By some estimates, Zambia could lose almost all its farms.

How likely is it? Pretty likely unless the world tackles both global warming and Africa's decline. Scientists agree that droughts will increase in a warmer world.

Acid Oceans

What could happen? The seas will gradually turn more and more acid. Coral reefs, shellfish and plankton, on which all life depends, will die off. Much of the life of the oceans will become extinct.

How would this come about? The oceans have absorbed half the carbon dioxide, the main cause of global warming, so far emitted by humanity. This forms dilute carbonic acid, which attacks corals and shells.

How likely is it? It is already starting. Scientists warn that the chemistry of the oceans is changing in ways unprecedented for 20 million years. Some predict that the world's coral reefs will die within 35 years.

Disease

What could happen? Malaria—which kills two million

people worldwide every year—reaches Britain with foreign travelers, gets picked up by British mosquitos and becomes endemic in the warmer climate.

How would this come about? Four of [Britain's] 40 mosquito species can carry the disease, and hundreds of travelers return with it annually. The insects breed faster, and feed more, in warmer temperatures.

How likely is it? A Department of Health study has suggested it may happen by 2050: the Environment Agency has mentioned 2020. Some experts say it is miraculous that it has not happened already.

Hurricanes

What could happen? Hurricanes, typhoons and violent storms proliferate, grow even fiercer, and hit new areas. September [2004's] repeated battering of Florida and the Caribbean may be just a foretaste of what is to come, say scientists.

How would this come about? The storms gather their energy from warm seas, and so, as oceans heat up, fiercer ones occur and threaten areas where at present the seas are too cool for such weather.

How likely is it? Scientists are divided over whether storms will get more frequent and whether the process has already begun.

"The political and journalistic doomsayers are wrong . . . there is no global warming problem."

Global Warming Does Not Pose a Serious Threat

John F. McManus

In the following viewpoint John F. McManus argues that dire warnings about global warming are raised by people who care more about increasing government regulations than about saving the Earth. In fact, he writes, claims about the supposed dangers of global warming ignore sound scientific arguments that there is no such problem. McManus claims that more carbon dioxide in the atmosphere is actually beneficial because it promotes plant growth. He also contends that the Earth experiences cold spells as well as heat waves, undermining the contention that the globe is getting hotter. McManus, a former engineer, is a member of the National Council of the John Birch Society, a conservative group that produces educational materials on a variety of subjects to help Americans achieve personal freedom and limited government.

As you read, consider the following questions:

1. As the author describes it, what is the purpose of the McCain-Lieberman proposal?
2. According to the author, why is an increase in atmospheric CO_2 desirable?
3. Why, in McManus's opinion, is the 2003 heat wave in France not a sign of global warming?

John F. McManus, "The Sky Is Falling! Or Is It?" *The New American*, vol. 19, September 8, 2003, p. 9. Copyright © 2003 by American Opinion Publishing, Inc. Reproduced by permission.

The steady stream of scary scenarios about global warming and its supposed cataclysmic consequences hasn't abated. It continues because its purveyors have an agenda that encompasses much more than environmental concerns. Those who insist that human beings, especially Americans, are endangering the future of mankind by causing the Earth's atmospheric temperature to rise ignore the many scientific refutations of their claims. What they seek is control of fellow man: how he lives, how he works, and whether constitutional limitations on his government shall endure. In their drive for power, they are regularly aided by elements of the Establishment media that also ignore sound science.

One significant example of the ongoing fright peddling is when Senators John McCain (R-Ariz.) and Joseph Lieberman (D-Conn.) managed to obtain a commitment from the full Senate that it will, before the year [2003] ends, consider their proposal to mandate controls on industrial emissions of carbon dioxide (CO_2). The two senators insist that atmospheric CO_2 must be reduced because it is the main cause of global warming. Predictably, Senator McCain argued that a voluntary approach to this problem wasn't acceptable because it did not "meet the urgency" of the threat. [The bill was considered, but rejected.]

Almost simultaneously, the governors of 10 northeastern states announced plans to spend the next two years developing a regional strategy to limit carbon emissions at coal- and oil-fired power plants in their areas. Their motive stemmed from the supposed need to combat global warming, a condition they too claim results from CO_2 being pumped into the atmosphere by man's burning of fossil fuels.

Applauding both of these developments, the *New York Times* editorialized that a great deal more must be done "to slow the warming trend" that is an "issue of great public concern on which the world has spoken clearly."

Many Scientists Question Global Warming

If leading politicians and the nation's leading newspaper agree that global warming is a serious problem, who dares to disagree? The answer is that a lengthening list of highly trained meteorologists, climatologists, geophysicists, and others in related scientific fields have, for decades, insisted that the political and journalistic doomsayers are wrong and that there is no global warming problem. These individuals continue to issue a stream of scientifically based responses that debunk the CO_2 and global warming scares. We present only some of their findings by posing questions of our own and letting trained experts supply answers. In some cases, we shall cite the absurdities supplied by the non-scientific doomsayers.

Has any senator risen to combat the McCain/Lieberman proposal?

On July 28th, [2003], Senator James Inhofe (R-Okla.), chairman of the Senate's Committee on Environment and Public Works, delivered an important speech attacking the claims of global warming alarmists and others who issue warnings about similarly unproved environmental threats. Senator Inhofe cited an array of scientific authorities to debunk the claims of "environmental extremists." He closed his remarks by urging colleagues to reject measures designed to treat nonexistent problems because they are "designed not to solve an environmental problem, but to satisfy the ever-growing demand of environmental groups for money and power. . . ."

What about the House of Representatives? Have its members been provided sound scientific perspective about carbon dioxide emissions and global warming?

On May 28, 2003, Dr. John R. Christy testified before the Committee on Resources of the U.S. House of Representatives. A professor of Atmospheric Science and director of the Earth System Science Center at the University of Alabama at Huntsville, Dr. Christy pointed out that carbon dioxide "is not a pollutant" and that its beneficial effect on plant life "is the lifeblood of the planet." Specifically addressing claims that CO_2 is causing planetary warming, Dr. Christy added: "Climate models suggest that the answer is yes; real data suggest otherwise." He is only one of a growing number to point to inaccuracies stemming from reliance on climate models intended to predict the weather many years in the future.

Addressing widespread insistence that man's activity has

caused recent warm weather, Dr. Christy, the recipient of awards from both NASA [National Aeronautics and Space Administration] and the American Meteorological Society, pointed to several studies indicating that "the climate we see today is not unusual at all." He noted that, in 2000, "the U.S. experienced the coldest combined November and December" in over 100 years and that "the 19 hottest summers in the past century occurred prior to 1955." He assured the House Committee members, "looking at these events does not prove the country is experiencing global cooling any more than a hot July represents global warming."

The Role of Carbon Dioxide

Does man's burning of fossil fuels actually account for most of the increased amount of CO_2 in the atmosphere?

The July [2003] issue of the Geological Society of America's *GSA Today* presented the results of independent studies conducted by a Canadian geologist and an Israeli astrophysicist. The two scientists agree that atmospheric CO_2 is rising, but they contend that interplay between solar activity and cosmic rays from deep space, not man's activity, is the chief cause of this increase. Jan Veizer of the University of Ottawa and Nir Shaviv of Hebrew University of Jerusalem had arrived at this conclusion independently of each other. The two met last October [2002] when they discovered their findings to be astoundingly similar. Their conclusions square with the claims of internationally renowned scientists Sallie Baliunas and Willie Soon, who have maintained for years that solar activity is the principal cause of climate fluctuations.

Is more CO_2 in the atmosphere actually a good development?

If healthy plant life is desirable, more CO_2 should be a goal because plants consume CO_2 just as animals (including humans) consume oxygen. Dr. Robert Balling, the director of climatology at Arizona State University, claims that increased CO_2, far from being harmful, is extremely beneficial. Referring to literature presented in publications produced for botanical scientists, Dr. Balling notes that there are "thousands of articles showing that elevated concentrations of CO_2 will be beneficial for plants." Dr. Balling cited experiments where plants grown with elevated levels of CO_2

were compared to similar plants grown without increasing the concentration of the supposedly dreaded gas. From New Zealand to America, the results reported in major peer-reviewed scientific journals are the same: Plants grown in the presence of additional CO_2 showed greater growth, less need for water, greater drought tolerance, and increased ability to deal with plant stresses. Instead of viewing CO_2 as a degrading pollutant, Dr. Balling urges fellow Americans to "drive out to the forest and feel good about the CO_2 coming out of your tailpipe!"

Didn't world leaders agree at 1997's UN-sponsored conference held in Kyoto, Japan, that industrialized nations must reduce CO_2 emissions to combat global warming?

Yes, delegates from many nations accepted the Kyoto Protocol, which would, according to the U.S. Energy Information Administration, cost the United States as much as $283 billion annually. But, as Cato Institute's Mario Lewis states, adopting the Kyoto guidelines "would have almost no effect on global temperatures." Basing his conclusions on the work of such eminent scientists as Massachusetts Institute of Technology's Dr. Richard Lindzen, Lewis maintains that forecasts of greater warming of the planet "are based on questionable climate history, implausible emission scenarios, and unconfirmed feedback effects." He urges Congress to reject "the flawed science and exaggerated claims of those who predict catastrophic global warming." Yet the House International Relations Committee recently approved a "Sense of the Congress" resolution introduced by Rep. Bob Menendez (D-N.J.) that advocates Kyoto-style suppression of domestic industrial activity to prevent impending climate catastrophe.

Other So-Called Evidence

Recent identical headlines in the New York Times *and* Los Angeles Times *claimed that "Arctic Ice Is Melting at Record Level." Doesn't this indicate global warming?*

Researchers from the Norwegian Polar Institute and the Norwegian Meteorological Institute have compiled data from ships' logs dating back five centuries. These entries show that the current "retreat of ice observed in the Arctic occurred previously, in the early 1700s." In an article appearing in the

Toronto Globe and Mail Chad Dick of the Arctic Climate Systems Study pointed to "natural cycles in sea ice extent" and stated that low levels of ice 300 years ago occurred before there were any significant man-made emissions of greenhouse gases such as CO_2. Also, the American Geophysical Union's *EOS* magazine published an article by Igor Polyakov who examined Arctic ice and temperature records from 1868 onward and found no evidence to back up those sensational claims.

No Cause for Alarm

Today, even saying there is scientific disagreement over global warming is itself controversial. But anyone who pays even cursory attention to the issue understands that scientists vigorously disagree over whether human activities are responsible for global warming, or whether those activities will precipitate natural disasters.

I would submit, furthermore, that not only is there a debate, but the debate is shifting away from those who subscribe to global warming alarmism. After studying the issue over the last several years, I believe that the balance of the evidence offers strong proof that natural variability is the overwhelming factor influencing climate.

It's also important to question whether global warming is even a problem for human existence. Thus far no one has seriously demonstrated any scientific proof that increased global temperatures would lead to the catastrophes predicted by alarmists. In fact, it appears that just the opposite is true: that increases in global temperatures may have a beneficial effect on how we live our lives.

U.S. Senator James M. Inhofe, "The Science of Climate Change," Senate Floor Statement, July 28, 2003.

Similarly, the January 2002 issue of *Science* magazine published the findings of scientists who, after measuring Antarctic ice formations, concluded that the ice near the South Pole is growing thicker. Another article appearing in *Nature* magazine pointed to the research led by scientist Peter Doran, who discovered temperatures in the Antarctic to have decreased, not increased, over the past 30 years. These scientific findings are among many that prompt Professor Patrick Michaels of the University of Virginia's Department of Environmental Sciences to chastise the "liberal media" for badly misleading the public on global warming.

How did the claims about global warming arise?

Dr. James Hansen of the National Aeronautics and Space Agency is reputed to be the godfather of the global warming scare. From his prominent position at NASA, he claimed in 1988 to be "99 percent sure" that man's activity was responsible for causing a rise in the Earth's temperature. But, by 1999, he backed off from his dire assessment and stated: "The forces that drive long-term climate change are not known with an accuracy sufficient to define future climate change." Yet advocates of larger and more intrusive government continue to present global warming as a threat and man's supposed role in causing it as a fact.

Reports coming out of Europe in mid-2003 pointed to a deadly heat wave. Isn't this an indication that global warming is a fact?

The summer heat wave throughout much of Europe was indeed severe, with France's Health Ministry reporting on August 14th that the heat wave killed as many as 3,000 people in France. But only seven months earlier, in January 2003, Europe experienced unusually cold weather. During this unusually cold period, a rare snowfall hit central London and more snow surprised southern France. Germany and central Europe were also hard hit with freezing temperatures, snow drifts, and transportation blockages.

In December 2002, a separate cold wave in northern India claimed the lives of 1,500 persons and won designation as one of the top five global catastrophes of 2002. Only a few years earlier, in November 1998, an Arctic cold wave swept into Europe and claimed scores of lives.

The promoters of global warming ignore repeatedly occurring cold spells. But competent scientists don't ignore them; they contend that sharp fluctuations in weather conditions, producing either hot or cold, occur because of nature and are to be expected.

There Is No Consensus

Have responsible scientists ever organized to challenge the claims about global warming and CO_2 emissions?

In 1998, a petition signed by more than 18,000 scientists sought to debunk the claims of global warming enthusiasts and even pointedly challenged the recommendations contained in the Kyoto Protocol. A letter from Dr. Frederick Seitz endorsing its content and an eight-page article reviewing the available research literature on the topic accompanied the widely circulated petition. When pressed, Dr. Seitz, a past president of the National Academy of Sciences, refused to remove his endorsement of the project. The accompanying article, written by physical chemist Dr. Arthur Robinson, stated that "predictions of harmful climatic effects due to future increases in minor greenhouse gases like carbon dioxide are in error and do not conform to current experimental knowledge."

The petition, signed by thousands of meteorologists, climatologists and atmospheric scientists, stated in part: "There is no convincing evidence that human release of carbon dioxide, methane, or other greenhouse gases is causing or will, in the foreseeable future, cause catastrophic heating of the Earth's atmosphere and disruption of the Earth's climate."

In a world plagued with terrorism and other crises, just how serious is the global warming problem supposed to be according to the environmentalists?

In July 2003, England's John Houghton, a former co-chairman of the highly politicized United Nations Intergovernmental Panel on Climate Change, said that he "had no hesitation" in describing global warming as "a weapon of mass destruction." Adding to his hyperbole, Houghton stated, "Like terrorism, this weapon knows no boundaries [and] can strike anywhere in any form—a heat wave in one place, a drought or a flood or a storm surge in another." According to this once-respected former chief of the British Meteorological Office, global warming "kills more people than terrorism."

Have any claimants about the danger of catastrophic global warming expressed any doubts about their theory?

Dr. Stephen Schneider of the National Center for Atmospheric Research was quoted by the October 1989 issue of *Discover* magazine as saying that scientists are "ethically bound . . . to tell the truth, the whole truth, and nothing but. . . ." So far, so good. Yet, after claiming that the earth faces "potentially disastrous climate change," he called on fellow global warming enthusiasts to "offer up scary scenarios, make simplified, dramatic statements, and make little mention of any doubts we might have." Compounding his willingness to deceive the public, he even suggested that colleagues had the option of choosing "between being effective and being honest."

What Environmentalists Really Want

What do these environmental extremists offer in place of the use of fossil fuels?

The "alternatives" usually advanced include solar, wind, and geothermal power. But the minuscule amounts of energy available from these alternative sources will never come close to matching the energy produced by coal, oil, and natural gas, the targeted fossil fuels. Indicative of the blindness and/or moral bankruptcy of most global warming enthusiasts is their almost universally negative attitude about safe, clean and efficient nuclear power.

Only a few weeks ago, however, a group of MIT [Massachusetts Institute of Technology] and Harvard scientists released a two-year study that boldly recommended increasing the number of America's nuclear power plants from 100 to 300. This is good news, even though the group accepts the false notion that carbon dioxide is "a greenhouse gas that contributes significantly to global warming."

What are the true goals of extreme environmentalists?

In 1972, Worldwatch Institute leader Lester Brown wrote that "an environmentally sustainable future requires nothing short of a revolution [that would include] restructuring the global economy, dramatically changing human reproductive behavior and altering values and lifestyles."

In 1991, Canadian billionaire Maurice Strong, poised to serve as the Secretary-General of the 1992 UN Earth Summit held in Rio de Janeiro, wrote: "It is clear that current lifestyles and consumption patterns of the affluent middle class . . . involving high meat intake, consumption of large amounts of frozen and 'convenience' foods, ownership of motor vehicles, numerous electric household appliances, home and workplace air conditioning . . . suburban housing . . . are not sustainable."

In his 1992 book *Earth in the Balance*, then-senator Al Gore insisted that "the effort to save the global environment" must become "the central organizing principle for every institution in society." He called for a "wrenching transformation" of society that must include "completely eliminating the internal combustion engine" because it is "the single greatest threat to our civilization." Not surprisingly, he never gave up using his own automobiles, each of which possesses one of those supposed threats to civilization under its hood.

In 1993, the UN released *Agenda 21: The Earth Summit Strategy to Save the Planet.* This massive blueprint for regimenting "every person on Earth" calls for "a profound reorientation of all human society." It calls for monitoring and controlling "the environmental consequences of every human action."

Many other examples could be cited showing that the real agenda behind the global-warming scare is about enchaining the planet, not saving it.

"Politicians, economists, journalists, and others may have the impression of confusion, disagreement, or discord among climate scientists, but that impression is incorrect."

Most Scientists Agree That Global Warming Is a Human-Caused Problem

Naomi Oreskes

A central question in the global warming debate is whether or not most scientists agree that in fact the Earth is getting hotter. In this viewpoint Naomi Oreskes reports on a study of articles published in scientific journals over a ten-year period. From this study, she claims, it is clear that within the scientific community nearly everyone agrees that global warming is real. These articles support the views of international environmental organizations such as the Intergovernmental Panel on Climate Change, which contend that human activities are leading to major climate change. Oreskes is a history professor at the University of California, San Diego, specializing in the historical development of scientific knowledge, methods, and practices.

As you read, consider the following questions:

1. According to the author, why might some people wish to believe that there is disagreement among scientists when it comes to global warming?
2. How many abstracts did Oreskes analyze for her study?
3. According to Oreskes, what still needs to be learned about climate change?

Naomi Oreskes, "The Scientific Consensus on Climate Change," *Science*, vol. 306, December 3, 2004, p. 1,686. Copyright © 2004 by the American Association for the Advancement of Science. Reproduced by permission.

Policy-makers and the media, particularly in the United States, frequently assert that climate science is highly uncertain. Some have used this as an argument against adopting strong measures to reduce greenhouse gas emissions. For example, while discussing a major U.S. Environmental Protection Agency report on the risks of climate change, then–EPA administrator Christine Whitman argued, "As [the report] went through review, there was less consensus on the science and conclusions on climate change." Some corporations whose revenues might be adversely affected by controls on carbon dioxide emissions have also alleged major uncertainties in the science. Such statements suggest that there might be substantive disagreement in the scientific community about the reality of anthropogenic climate change. This is not the case.

The scientific consensus is clearly expressed in the reports of the Intergovernmental Panel on Climate Change (IPCC). Created in 1988 by the World Meteorological Organization and the United Nations Environmental Programme, IPCC's purpose is to evaluate the state of climate science as a basis for informed policy action, primarily on the basis of peer-reviewed and published scientific literature. In its most recent assessment. IPCC states unequivocally that the consensus of scientific opinion is that Earth's climate is being affected by human activities: "Human activities . . . are modifying the concentration of atmospheric constituents . . . that absorb or scatter radiant energy. . . . Most of the observed warming over the last 50 years is likely to have been due to the increase in greenhouse gas concentrations."

Scientific Bodies Agree

IPCC is not alone in its conclusions. In recent years, all major scientific bodies in the United States whose members' expertise bears directly on the matter have issued similar statements. For example, the National Academy of Sciences report, *Climate Change Science: An Analysis of Some Key Questions*, begins: "Greenhouse gases are accumulating in Earth's atmosphere as a result of human activities, causing surface air temperatures and subsurface ocean temperatures to rise." The report explicitly asks whether the IPCC assessment is a fair summary of professional scientific thinking, and answers yes: "The IPCC's conclusion that most of the observed warming of the last 50 years is likely to have been due to the increase in greenhouse gas concentrations accurately reflects the current thinking of the scientific community on this issue."

A Strong Consensus

If you look at all the peer-reviewed work of people who are researching various aspects of the climate, there is virtually no research that has been peer reviewed that says this is not happening. And so there is a very strong consensus, and . . . , this IPCC [Intergovernmental Panel on Climate Change] looks at the work of more than 2,000 scientists from 100 countries, and they conclude that there is really no challenge to the larger trends. There are disputes about a lot of second-level questions. There are disputes about the rates of future warming, about specific impacts in geographical regions, about the role of clouds, for example, some clouds reflect heat, some clouds trap in heat, but in terms of the larger trends, there is a consensus, there is no dispute among any real credentialed scientists about what is happening and even Dr [Richard] Lindzen acknowledges it's happening. He just sort of dismisses it as being negligible.

Ross Gelbspan, interviewed by Tony Jones, *Lateline*, July 3, 2005. www.abc.net.au.

Others agree. The American Meteorological Society, the American Geophysical Union, and the American Association for the Advancement of Science (AAAS) all have issued statements in recent years concluding that the evidence for human modification of climate is compelling.

Journal Articles Agree

The drafting of such reports and statements involves many opportunities for comment, criticism, and revision, and it is not likely that they would diverge greatly from the opinions of the societies' members. Nevertheless, they might downplay legitimate dissenting opinions. That hypothesis was tested by analyzing 928 abstracts, published in refereed scientific journals between 1993 and 2003, and listed in the ISI [Institute for Scientific Information] database with the keywords "[global] climate change."

The 928 papers were divided into six categories: explicit endorsement of the consensus position, evaluation of impacts, mitigation proposals, methods, paleoclimate analysis, and rejection of the consensus position. Of all the papers, 75% fell into the first three categories, either explicitly or implicitly accepting the consensus view; 25% dealt with methods or paleoclimate, taking no position on current anthropogenic climate change. Remarkably, none of the papers disagreed with the consensus position.

Admittedly, authors evaluating impacts, developing methods, or studying paleoclimatic change might believe that current climate change is natural. However, none of these papers argued that point.

This analysis shows that scientists publishing in the peer-reviewed literature agree with IPCC, the National Academy of Sciences, and the public statements of their professional societies. Politicians, economists, journalists, and others may have the impression of confusion, disagreement, or discord among climate scientists, but that impression is incorrect.

The scientific consensus might, of course, be wrong. If the history of science teaches anything, it is humility, and no one can be faulted for failing to act on what is not known. But our grandchildren will surely blame us if they find that we understood the reality of anthropogenic climate change and failed to do anything about it.

Many details about climate interactions are not well understood, and there are ample grounds for continued research to provide a better basis for understanding climate dynamics. The question of what to do about climate change is also still open. But there is a scientific consensus on the reality of anthropogenic climate change. Climate scientists have repeatedly tried to make this clear. It is time for the rest of us to listen.

*"Even a rudimentary survey of scientific
literature reveals there to be very little
agreement on the subject of climate change."*

Many Scientists Do Not Agree
That Global Warming Is a
Human-Caused Problem

Greening Earth Society

In the following viewpoint the Greening Earth Society argues that there is no consensus about global warming in the
scientific community, contrary to what many environmentalists claim. For example, the viewpoint notes, a chart that
shows constant temperatures over centuries with a sudden
increase over the past fifty years, called the "hockey stick"
because of the shape of its curve, is often thought to be universally accepted by scientists, when actually many question
its validity. Moreover, according to the society, scientists do
not agree that human activity causes whatever warming does
occur. The Greening Earth Society, sponsored by electric
companies and their suppliers, publishes articles that challenge the idea that emissions of carbon dioxide will lead to
catastrophic climate change.

As you read, consider the following questions:

1. In the authors' view, what is the weakness in Naomi
   Oreskes's claim about consensus and global warming?
2. According to Hans von Storch, what charges were leveled
   against those who challenged the "hockey stick" curve?
3. What is one idea around which there is "undeniable
   scientific consensus," according to this viewpoint?

Greening Earth Society, "Global Warming Consensus," www.co2andclimate.org,
January 14, 2005. Copyright © 2005 by the Greening Earth Society. Reproduced
by permission.

The phrase "scientific consensus" suggests something approaching unanimous agreement among scientists. However even a rudimentary survey of scientific literature reveals there to be very little agreement on the subject of climate change. The unfortunate and inaccurate characterization of consensus is used as a rhetorical bludgeon of skeptics and is the basis of a push for industrialized nations to "do something" to reduce the atmosphere's greenhouse gas concentration.

Dr. Richard Lindzen of the Massachusetts Institute of Technology offered an explanation of the phenomenon during a recent National Press Club briefing "Climate Alarm—Where does it come from?":

> With respect to science, consensus is often simply a sop to scientific illiteracy. After all, if what you are told is alleged to be supported by all scientists, then why do you have to bother to understand it? You can simply go back to treating it as a matter of religious belief, and you never have to defend this belief except to claim that you are supported by all scientists except for a handful of corrupted heretics.

No Consensus on Human Causes

The theme of scientific consensus creeps into documents such as the *Arctic Climate Impact Assessment Overview Report* (2004) and the UN Intergovernmental Panel on Climate Change's (IPCC) *Third Assessment Report* (2001). A good example of how this plays out was demonstrated in the December 3, 2004 edition of *Science* in which University of California–San Diego's Naomi Oreskes warns readers, "[O]ur grandchildren will surely blame us if they find that we understood the reality of anthropogenic climate change and failed to do anything about it."

We understood the *reality?* What's the basis of her claim? The IPCC "states unequivocally that the consensus of scientific opinion is that Earth is being affected by human activities," she writes. She goes on to specify that the IPCC concludes, "[M]ost of the observed warming over the last 50 years is likely to have been due to the increase in greenhouse gas concentrations." Those statements suffer a serious shortcoming; our grandchildren will need only study the scientific literature available to their grandparents to discover that, in fact, neither the IPCC nor a particular scientist has convincingly demonstrated how human-caused contributions to atmospheric greenhouse gases are responsible for "most" of the observed warming over the past fifty years.

To highlight the difficulty of reaching true scientific consensus, one need only consider the infamous 1,000-year temperature history prominently featured in the 2001 IPCC *Third Assessment Report* (TAR). It re-appeared in the 2004 *Arctic Climate Impact Assessment* (ACIA) *Overview Report* and is a perfect example of the complex challenge of achieving quantitative understanding of the earth's climate system. The "hockey stick curve" [where Earth's temperature remains constant over many centuries then suddenly increases] was almost unanimously hailed as a scientific consensus that strongly suggests the exceptional nature of temperature change in the last fifty years. But it wasn't long before independent-minded scientists and researchers discovered holes in the theory. That fact alone invalidates the claim of consensus.

One of them, Professor Hans von Storch, who directs the Institute of Coastal Research at Geesthacht, Germany, recently remarked on "the ethical implications of the premature acceptance of the 'hockey stick' by the scientific community." He writes:

> When we recently established that the method behind the so-called "hockey stick" curve of Northern Hemisphere temperature is flawed, this result was not so much attacked as scientifically flawed but was seen both in private conversations and public discourse as outright dangerous, because it could be instrumentalized and undermine the success of the IPCC process. . . .

We note that Von Storch and his co-authors followed with an aside that "the concept of anthropogenic climate change is compelling even if the hockey-stick curve is false." That kind of statement further confirms the dangerous implications of the constant invocation of scientific consensus.

Consensus: Models Are Unreliable

One thing about which there is undeniable scientific consensus is the difficulty even the most sophisticated climate models face in deciding on the impact of clouds under the familiar scenario of doubling the atmospheric carbon diox-

Thousands Say Humans Are Not the Cause

Over 17,000 scientists have signed a petition saying, in part, "there is no convincing scientific evidence that human release of carbon dioxide, methane, or other greenhouse gases is causing or will, in the foreseeable future, cause catastrophic heating of the Earth's atmosphere and disruption of the Earth's climate."

The petition is being circulated by the Oregon Institute of Science and Medicine, an independent research organization that receives no funding from industry. Among the signers of the petition are over 2,100 physicists, geophysicsts, climatologists, meteorologists, and environmental scientists who are especially well-qualified to evaluate the effects of carbon dioxide on the Earth's atmosphere. Another 4,400 signers are scientists qualified to comment on carbon dioxide's effects on plant and animal life. Nearly all of the signers have some sort of advanced technical training.

The qualifications of the signers of the Oregon Institute Petition are dramatically better than the 2,600 "scientists" who have signed a competing petition calling for immediate action to counter global warming. More than 90 percent of that petition's signers lacked credentials to speak with authority on the issue. The entire list included just *one* climatologist.

Over one hundred climate scientists signed the 1996 Leipzig Declaration, which stated in part, "there does not exist today a general scientific consensus about the importance of greenhouse warming from rising levels of carbon dioxide. On the contrary, most scientists now accept the fact that actual observations from earth satellites show no climate warming whatsoever."

A survey of 36 state climatologists—scientists retained by state governments to monitor and research climate issues—conducted in 1997 found that 58 percent disagreed with the statement, "global warming is for real," while only 36 percent agreed. A remarkable 89 percent agreed that "current science is unable to isolate and measure variations in global temperatures caused only by man-made factors."

Jack L. Bast, "Instant Expert Guide: Global Warming," www.heartland.org, 1998.

---

ide concentration. . . . Models produc[e] contradictory results. The discredited U.S. National Assessment suffered from such chicanery. . . . Depending on which climate model you examine, any one of three combinations of increased, decreased, or little or no change in future cloud cover is assumed. This places modelers in a very awkward position if they suggest an ability to predict future climate. If nearly any tendency is possible, the models are incapable of making a reliable prediction. Such a devastating realization should—scientifically speaking—stop cold all the what-if scenarios commonly used to justify the need for immediate, drastic cuts in CO_2 emissions.

The difficulty and ambiguity of determining what could happen to the cloud field under an enhanced greenhouse effect easily can be appreciated in this latest review [by Tjernstrom and others] of the state-of-the-art modeling of Arctic clouds:

> Correct radiation at the surface requires a correct cloud field, which is far from trivial. . . . A cursory look at the liquid water path reveals that the models mostly do reasonably well, except during winter when the observations reveal substantial liquid water while models almost entirely have ice-only clouds. . . . On average, the modeled bias in net radiation is about -10 [Watts per meter squared], however, the net errors in the individual models range from –44 to 5 [Watts per meter squared]. More serious is the fact that the net errors in the different models come from different components of the radiation budget. In some models, errors in incoming and outgoing radiation compensate, but in others they reinforce. It is quite possible that the balance between the terms in the net radiation budget shifts in a changed climate. Thus using these formulations in a climate model, the net-radiation errors may shift in a quite unpredictable manner. . . .

The Arctic researchers . . . explained how, according to Arctic cloud observations utilizing both radar and lidar during the so-called SHEBA (Surface Heat Budget of the Arctic Ocean project) campaign, liquid water was detected for clouds as high as 6.5 km and at temperatures 34°C below the freezing point for water. They further note, "Moreover, none of the [six] models consider Arctic haze or indirect effects of aerosol particles."

Consensus: Aerosols Are Not Understood

Another emergent scientific consensus concerns lack of understanding of the climatic impacts of both anthropogenic and natural aerosols. Early on, Gary Russell and colleagues

... of NASA's Goddard Institute for Space Studies cautioned "[o]ne danger of adding aerosols of unknown strength and location is that they can be tuned to give more accurate comparisons with current observations but cover up model deficiencies."

More recently, Theodore Anderson and colleagues . . . issued several strong cautions in *Science:*

> [W]e argue that the magnitude and uncertainty of aerosol forcing may affect the magnitude and uncertainty of total forcing [i.e., "the global mean sum of all industrial-era forcings"] to a degree that has not been adequately considered in climate studies to date. Inferences about the causes of surface warming over the industrial period and about climate sensitivity may therefore be in error. . . . Unfortunately, virtually all climate model studies that have included anthropogenic aerosol forcing as a driver of climate change (diagnosis, attribution, and projection studies; denoted "applications" in the figure) have used only aerosol forcing values that are consistent with the inverse approach. If such studies were conducted with the larger range of aerosol forcings determined from the forward calculations, the results would differ greatly. The forward calculations raise the possibility that total forcing from preindustrial times to the present . . . has been small or even negative. If this is correct, it would imply that climate sensitivity and/or natural variability (that is, variability not forced by anthropogenic emissions) is much larger than climate models currently indicate. . . . In addressing the critical question of how the climate system will respond to this [anthropogenic greenhouse gas] positive forcing, researchers must seek to resolve the present disparity between forward and inverse calculations. Until this is achieved, the possibility that most of the warming to date is due to natural variability, as well as the possibility of high climate sensitivity, must be kept open. . . .

For those involved in impact assessments of future climate change, James Hansen . . . of NASA Goddard Institute for Space Studies warns of clear exaggeration of the CO_2 emission scenarios adopted by the IPCC:

> One problem with IPCC reports is that each report produces new (and more numerous) greenhouse gas scenarios with little attempt to discuss what went wrong with the previous ones. As a result, dramatic changes that have occurred since the 1980s in prospects for future climate forcings receive inadequate attention. . . . CO_2 scenarios are the most critical.

We note that growth rate of CO_2 (fossil fuel) emissions has declined from about 4% per year to 1% per year in recent decades. It is noteworthy that the current IPCC (2001) scenarios have a growth rate in the 1990s that is almost double the observed rate of 0.8%/year . . . but it is consistent with their failure to emphasize data. . . .

In other words, the IPCC emission-scenario team fails to account for the relatively lower and slower rates of emission trends. They do not account for the observed tendencies.

On these varied bases, there *should be* clear scientific consensus that the IPCC or ACIA CO_2 emission scenarios for the future are biased, exaggerated and/or uncertain. Instead, Naomi Oreskes and others cite the "consensus of scientists" the IPCC or ACIA supposedly represents. In Dick Lindzen's words, that's a sop to scientific illiteracy.

Periodical Bibliography

The following articles have been selected to supplement the diverse views presented in this chapter.

Lee Ann Fisher Baron   "'Junk Science': The Need for Science Education," *Current*, January 2001.

Steven Brockerman   "The Myth of Catastrophic Global Warming," *Capitalism Magazine*, August 29, 2002. www.capmag.com.

Michael Crichton   "Take the Fiction Out of Science Policy," *American Enterprise*, June 2005.

Tim Dickinson   "Diary of a Dying Planet," *Rolling Stone*, June 10, 2004.

Michael Hanlon   "There's No Time Like the Present," *Spectator*, August 7, 2004.

Mari N. Jensen   "Consensus on Ecological Impacts Remains Elusive," *Science*, January 3, 2003.

Richard A. Kerr   "Dueling Models: Future U.S. Climate Uncertain," *Science*, June 23, 2000.

Mark LaRochelle and Peter Spencer   "'Global Warming' Science: Fact vs. Fiction," *Consumers' Research Magazine*, July 2001.

Patrick J. Michaels   "Extreme Weather: And Extremely Bad Logic!" *UN Chronicle*, December 2002–February 2003.

Kathleen Parker   "Let Logic Join the Global Warming Debate," *USA Today*, May 3, 2005.

Fred Pearce   "Meltdown!" *New Scientist*, November 2, 2002. www.newscientist.com.

Roddy Scheer   "Changing the Climate," *E: The Environmental Magazine*, January/February 2005.

Mikhail Skafidas   "Global Warming as Big a Threat as WMD," *New Perspectives Quarterly*, Summer 2004.

Constanza Villalba   "From Tree Rings to Ice Cores," *Weatherwise*, September/October 2000.

CHAPTER 2

What Causes Global Warming?

Chapter Preface

Many scientists agree that the Earth's temperature appears to have increased about one degree Fahrenheit during the twentieth century. Scientists report that the 1990s was the hottest decade since temperatures have been recorded, and evidence of warming appears in everything from thinning of ice sheets to increasingly severe weather. But scientists do not agree about what is causing the apparent warming, or about whether it can be stopped.

Many climatologists believe that carbon dioxide (CO_2) in the atmosphere is the primary cause of global warming, but even among those scientists there is a debate about whether the carbon dioxide is anthropogenic (caused by humans) or naturally occurring. Some argue that carbon emissions have increased dramatically since the Industrial Revolution, and that the warming trend can be traced back to that period. The Intergovernmental Panel on Climate Change, for example, argues that there has been a "discernible human influence" on climate. But scientists studying ancient climates through ice core samples report that the Earth has had many periods of warming and cooling in its 4-billion-year history, reaching back far before humans started introducing carbon dioxide into the atmosphere in significant amounts. As scientist Jens Bischof points out, "Natural climate changes occur as well as manmade ones." And studies of the impact of methane gas (CH_4) emissions provide evidence that the methane released through the production and transport of coal, and through the natural emissions of cows and of rotting peat bogs, share responsibility for global warming.

Causes that do not depend on emissions are also being studied. Writer Richard Kerr explains that "the sun has shown intriguing hints at variability that suggest that it could play a role in altering terrestrial temperatures," but it is not yet known how strong the sun-climate connection might be. Fluctuations in the saltiness of the oceans, cyclical wind patterns, radiation from the Earth's core, and changes in the way humans use land are all considered possible causes of climate change.

Ironically, studies released in May 2005 indicate that efforts to reduce smog and other pollutants over the past quarter century may contribute to global warming. Thirty years ago, while carbon dioxide and other greenhouse gases were trapping the sun's heat within the atmosphere, large amounts of other pollutants blocked some of the sun's rays from reaching Earth in the first place. Now that massive efforts to reduce smog have taken effect, particularly in the former Soviet Union, climatologists believe that more heat reaches the Earth, resulting in higher temperatures.

No one disputes that climate is complicated, shaped by many variables. In the following chapter authors present a range of opinions about those variables and which of them might be most responsible for global warming.

*"Over the past 50 years, human influences
have been the dominant detectable
influence on climate change."*

Human Activity Causes Global Warming

Thomas R. Karl and Kevin E. Trenberth

While global climate change is due in part to natural fluctuations in the Earth's temperature, human activity has become the most significant influence, argue Thomas R. Karl and Kevin E. Trenberth in the following viewpoint. According to these scientists, greenhouse gas emissions from the burning of fossil fuels have led to a warming of the atmosphere, which in turn has altered both regional and global climate. These human-caused changes are likely to be long-lasting, the scientists conclude. Karl is director of the National Climate Data Center at the National Oceanic and Atmospheric Administration, and Trenberth is head of the Climate Analysis Section at the National Center for Atmospheric Research.

As you read, consider the following questions:

1. What is one natural cause of interference with the Earth's energy flows, as described by the authors?
2. How much has the amount of carbon dioxide in the atmosphere increased since preindustrial times, as cited by the authors?
3. According to Karl and Trenberth, will the magnitude of human-induced climate change increase or decrease in the future?

Thomas R. Karl and Kevin E. Trenberth, "Modern Global Climate Change," *Science*, vol. 302, December 5, 2003, p. 1,719. Copyright © 2003 by the American Association for the Advancement of Science. Reproduced by permission.

The atmosphere is a global commons that responds to many types of emissions into it, as well as to changes in the surface beneath it. As human balloon flights around the world illustrate, the air over a specific location is typically halfway around the world a week later, making climate change a truly global issue.

Planet Earth is habitable because of its location relative to the sun and because of the natural greenhouse effect of its atmosphere. Various atmospheric gases contribute to the greenhouse effect, whose impact in clear skies is ~60% from water vapor, ~25% from carbon dioxide, ~8% from ozone, and the rest from trace gases including methane and nitrous oxide. Clouds also have a greenhouse effect. On average, the energy from the sun received at the top of the Earth's atmosphere amounts to 175 petawatts (PW) (or 175 quadrillion watts), of which ~31% is reflected by clouds and from the surface. The rest (120 PW) is absorbed by the atmosphere, land, or ocean and ultimately emitted back to space as infrared radiation. Over the past century, infrequent volcanic eruptions of gases and debris into the atmosphere have significantly perturbed these energy flows; however, the resulting cooling has lasted for only a few years. Inferred changes in total solar irradiance appear to have increased global mean temperatures by perhaps as much as 0.2°C in the first half of the 20th century, but measured changes in the past 25 years are small. Over the past 50 years, human influences have been the dominant detectable influence on climate change. The following briefly describes the human influences on climate, [and] the resulting temperature and precipitation changes. . . .

Humans Have Changed the Atmosphere's Composition

The main way in which humans alter global climate is by interference with the natural flows of energy through changes in atmospheric composition, not by the actual generation of heat in energy usage. On a global scale, even a 1% change in the energy flows, which is the order of the estimated change to date, dominates all other direct influences humans have on climate. For example, an energy output of just one PW is equivalent to that of a million power stations of 1000-MW capacity, among the largest in the world. Total human energy use is about a factor of 9000 less than the natural flow.

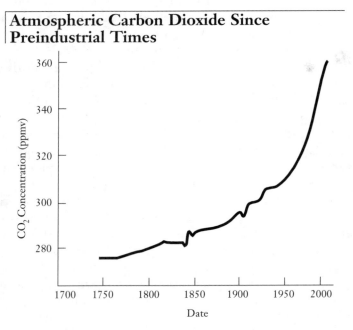

Atmospheric Carbon Dioxide Since Preindustrial Times

Atmospheric carbon dioxide has increased from a value of about 275 parts per million before the Industrial Revolution to about 360 parts per million in 1996, and the rate of increase has speeded up over this span of time.

University Corporation for Atmospheric Research, *Our Changing Climate: Reports to the Nation*, Fall 1997.

Global changes in atmospheric composition occur from anthropogenic [human-caused] emissions of greenhouse gases, such as carbon dioxide that results from the burning of fossil fuels and methane and nitrous oxide from multiple human activities. Because these gases have long (decades to centuries) atmospheric lifetimes, the result is an accumulation in the atmosphere and a buildup in concentrations that are clearly shown both by instrumental observations of air samples since 1958 and in bubbles of air trapped in ice cores before then. Moreover, these gases are well distributed in the atmosphere across the globe, simplifying a global monitoring strategy. Carbon dioxide has increased 31% since preindustrial times, from 280 parts per million by volume (ppmv) to more than 370 ppmv today, and half of the increase has been since 1965. The greenhouse gases trap outgoing radiation from the Earth to space, creating a warming of the planet.

Emissions into the atmosphere from fuel burning further result in gases that are oxidized to become highly reflective micron-sized aerosols, such as sulfate, and strongly absorbing aerosols, such as black carbon or soot. Aerosols are rapidly (within a week or less) removed from the atmosphere through the natural hydrological cycle and dry deposition as they travel away from their source. Nonetheless, atmospheric concentrations can substantially exceed background conditions in large areas around and downwind of the emission sources. Depending on their reflectivity and absorption properties, geometry and size distribution, and interactions with clouds and moisture, these particulates can lead to either net cooling, as for sulfate aerosols, or net heating, as for black carbon. Importantly, sulfate aerosols affect climate directly by reflecting solar radiation and indirectly by changing the reflective properties of clouds and their lifetimes. Understanding their precise impact has been hampered by our inability to measure these aerosols directly, as well as by their spatial inhomogeneity [size differences] and rapid changes in time. Large-scale measurements of aerosol patterns have been inferred through emission data, special field experiments, and indirect measurements such as sun photometers.

Humans Have Changed Land-Use Patterns

Human activities also have a large-scale impact on the land surface. Changes in land-use through urbanization and agricultural practices, although not global, are often most pronounced where people live, work, and grow food, and are part of the human impact on climate. Large-scale deforestation and desertification in Amazonia and the Sahel, respectively, are two instances where evidence suggests there is likely to be human influence on regional climate. In general, city climates differ from those in surrounding rural green areas, because of the "concrete jungle" and its effects on heat retention, runoff, and pollution, resulting in urban heat islands.

There is no doubt that the composition of the atmosphere is changing because of human activities, and today greenhouse gases are the largest human influence on global climate. Recent greenhouse gas emission trends in the United States are upward, as are global emissions trends, with increases between 0.5 and 1% per year over the past few decades. Concentrations of both reflective and nonreflective aerosols are also estimated to be increasing. Because radiative forcing from greenhouse gases dominates over the net cooling forcings from aerosols, the popular term for the human influence on global climate is "global warming," although it really means global heating, of which the observed global temperature increase is only one consequence. Already it is estimated that the Earth's climate has exceeded the bounds of natural variability, and this has been the case since about 1980.

Surface moisture, if available (as it always is over the oceans), effectively acts as the "air conditioner" of the surface, as heat used for evaporation moistens the air rather than warming it. Therefore, another consequence of global heating of the lower troposphere is accelerated land-surface drying and more atmospheric water vapor (the dominant greenhouse gas). Accelerated drying increases the incidence and severity of droughts, whereas additional atmospheric water vapor increases the risk of heavy precipitation events. Basic theory, climate model simulations, and empirical evidence all confirm that warmer climates, owing to increased water vapor, lead to more intense precipitation events even when the total precipitation remains constant, and with prospects for even stronger events when precipitation amounts increase.

Human Influence Is Increasing

There is considerable uncertainty as to exactly how anthropogenic global heating will affect the climate system, how long it will last, and how large the effects will be. Climate has varied naturally in the past, but today's circumstances are unique because of human influences on atmospheric composition. As we progress into the future, the magnitude of the present anthropogenic change will become overwhelmingly large compared to that of natural changes. In the absence of climate mitigation policies, the 90% probability interval for warming from 1990 to 2100 is 1.7° to 4.9°C. About half of this range is due to uncertainty in future emissions and about half is due to uncertainties in climate models, especially in their sensitivity to forcings that are complicated by feedbacks . . . and in their rate of heat uptake by the oceans. Even with these uncertainties, the likely outcome is more frequent heat waves, droughts, extreme precipitation events, and related impacts (such as wild fires, heat stress, vegetation changes, and sea level rise) that will be regionally dependent.

The rate of human-induced climate change is projected to be much faster than most natural processes, certainly those prevailing over the past 10,000 years. Thresholds likely exist that, if crossed, could abruptly and perhaps almost irreversibly switch the climate to a different regime. Such rapid change is evident in past climates during a slow change in the Earth's orbit and tilt, such as the Younger Dryas cold event from ~11,500 to ~12,700 years ago, perhaps caused by freshwater discharges from melting ice sheets into the North Atlantic Ocean and a change in the ocean thermohaline [salt] circulation. The great ice sheets of Greenland and Antarctica may not be stable, because the extent to which cold-season heavier snowfall partially offsets increased melting as the climate warms remains uncertain. A combination of ocean temperature increases and ice sheet melting could systematically inundate the world's coasts by raising sea level for centuries.

Given what has happened to date and is projected in the future, substantial further climate change is guaranteed. The rate of change can be slowed, but it is unlikely to be stopped in the 21st century. Because concentrations of long-lived greenhouse gases are dominated by accumulated past emissions, it takes many decades for any change in emissions to have much effect. This means the atmosphere still has unrealized warming (estimated to be at least another 0.5°C) and that sea level rise may continue for centuries after an abatement of anthropogenic [human-caused] greenhouse gas emissions and the stabilization of greenhouse gas concentrations in the atmosphere.

*"Human kind has little or nothing to do
with the recent temperature changes."*

Human Activity Does Not Cause Global Warming

William M. Gray

Natural variations in the degree of saltiness of the oceans lead in turn to variations in global ocean currents. In this viewpoint William M. Gray argues that these natural variations are the cause of periodic global temperature increases. Attributing global warming to human activities such as the burning of fossil fuels, Gray concludes, is evidence of a misunderstanding about the natural fluctuations that have always occurred. An expert on tropical meteorology, Gray is a professor of atmospheric science at Colorado State University.

As you read, consider the following questions:
1. What happened to surface temperatures between the mid-1940s and the early 1970s, according to Gray?
2. As the author explains it, what is a positive feedback loop?
3. Why, according to Gray, might scientists be willing to "bend their objectivity" and exaggerate or misuse scientific knowledge?

As a boy, I remember seeing articles about the large global warming that had taken place between 1900 and 1945. No one understood or knew if this warming would continue. Then the warming abated and I heard little about such warming through the late 1940s and into the 1970s.

In fact, surface measurements showed a small global cooling between the mid-1940s and the early 1970s. During the 1970s, there was speculation concerning an increase in this cooling. Some speculated that a new ice age may not be far off.

Then in the 1980s, it all changed again. The current global warming bandwagon that US-European governments have been alarming us with is still in full swing.

Not Our Fault

Are we, the fossil-fuel-burning public, partially responsible for this recent warming trend? Almost assuredly not.

These small global temperature increases of the last 25 years and over the last century are likely natural changes that the globe has seen many times in the past.

This small warming is likely a result of the natural alterations in global ocean currents which are driven by ocean salinity variations. Ocean circulation variations are as yet little understood.

Human kind has little or nothing to do with the recent temperature changes. We are not that influential.

There is a negative or complementary nature to human-induced greenhouse gas increases in comparison with the dominant natural greenhouse gas of water vapour and its cloud derivatives.

It has been assumed by the human-induced global warming advocates that as anthropogenic [human-made] greenhouse gases increase, water vapour and upper-level cloudiness will also rise and lead to accelerated warming—a positive feedback loop.

It is not the human-induced greenhouse gases themselves which cause significant warming but the assumed extra water vapour and cloudiness that some scientists hypothesise.

The global general circulation models which simulate significant amounts of human-induced warming are incorrectly structured to give this positive feedback loop. Their internal model assumptions are thus not realistic.

As greenhouse gases rise, global-averaged upper-level atmospheric water vapour and thin cirrus [clouds] should be expected to decrease, not increase.

Has the Earth Warmed?

With a reluctant nod to the Clinton administration, [the] seemingly simple question [Has the Earth Warmed?] depends upon what the definitions of "has" and "earth" are. Depending upon that definition, we can answer yes, no, or do not know. Why? Because the earth's temperature is hardly constant. The earth has warmed and cooled for billions of years, and the current ice-age regime is one of the most variable periods in that inconstant history. It is an astounding fact to behold that this planet is around five billion years old but has likely seen large areas of glacial ice for only around one half of 1 percent (a crude estimate at best) of its total history.

This Ice Age is hardly over. We are merely between glacial phases; indeed, we are due for a reglaciation, if the history of the last million years or so is any guide.

The Ice Age Earth is a planet whose temperature fluctuates wildly, and we just happen to be here during that era, cheerily emitting compounds into the atmosphere that are themselves known to change the surface temperature. Finding the human fingerprint on an atmosphere at the height of chaos is a daunting task indeed.

Patrick J. Michaels and Robert C. Balling Jr., *The Satanic Gases*, 2000.

Water vapour and cirrus cloudiness should be thought of as a negative rather than a positive feedback to human-induced —or anthropogenic—greenhouse gas increases.

No significant human-induced greenhouse gas warming can occur with such a negative feedback loop.

Climate Debate Has "Life of Its Own"

Our global climate's temperature has always fluctuated back and forth and it will continue to do so, irrespective of how much or how little greenhouse gases we put into the atmosphere.

Although initially generated by honest scientific questions of how human-produced greenhouse gases might affect global climate, this topic has now taken on a life of its own.

It has been extended and grossly exaggerated and misused by those wishing to make gain from the exploitation of ignorance on this subject.

This includes the governments of developed countries, the media and scientists who are willing to bend their objectivity to obtain government grants for research on this topic.

I have closely followed the carbon dioxide warming arguments. From what I have learned of how the atmosphere ticks over 40 years of study, I have been unable to convince myself that a doubling of human-induced greenhouse gases can lead to anything but quite small and insignificant amounts of global warming.

"SUVs have a dark side. They spew out 43 percent more global-warming pollution and 47 percent more air pollution than an average car."

Sport Utility Vehicles Contribute to Global Warming

Sierra Club

Sport utility vehicles (SUVs) contribute significantly to pollution and global warming, according to the following viewpoint from the Sierra Club. Because they emit more carbon dioxide than do cars, SUVs contribute more to the greenhouse effect, which raises the temperature of the Earth. Although the technology exists to improve SUVs, the organization argues, Congress has bowed to pressure from automobile manufacturers and refused to require SUVs to be safer, cleaner, and more fuel-efficient. The Sierra Club is one of the oldest and largest environmental advocacy groups in the United States.

As you read, consider the following questions:
1. Why, according to the authors, are SUVs not held to the same environmental standards as passenger cars?
2. According to the authors, what percentage of the carbon dioxide pollution created in the United States is caused by cars and light trucks?
3. According to the Sierra Club, do new vehicles today use more or less fuel than new vehicles in 1980, on average?

W hen it comes to wasting energy, SUVs are unrivaled. Built with outdated, gas-guzzling technology, many SUVs get just 13 miles per gallon. And the higher gas prices are, the more money they waste.

Auto-industry advertising portrays SUVs as the ticket to freedom and the great outdoors. Commercials depict them climbing massive snow-capped mountains or tearing through desert sand dunes, taking their owners into the wild. In reality, the only off-road action many of these vehicles see is accidentally driving through a flower bed next to the driveway.

Missing from these ads are other contributions from SUVs—the brown haze of air pollution hanging over many of our national parks, images of weather disasters linked to global warming or the oil derricks and tankers needed to feed gas-guzzling SUVs. In contrast to Detroit's carefully crafted image, SUVs have a dark side. They spew out 43 percent more global-warming pollution and 47 percent more air pollution than an average car. SUVs are four times more likely than cars to roll over in an accident and three times more likely to kill the occupants in a rollover. They also cost the owner thousands more in gasoline.

Worsening the Threat of Global Warming

Because the government classifies SUVs as "light trucks" rather than cars, SUVs have a license to guzzle more gas and pollute more than cars. In 1975, when fuel-economy standards were first adopted, "light truck" referred to a vehicle used to haul hay on the farm or gravel at a construction site. At that time, light trucks comprised only 20 percent of the vehicle market. Today, SUVs, mini-vans and other light trucks make up nearly half of new vehicles sold. They are far more likely to haul lattés home from Starbucks than lumber from the yard. Even though Detroit has technology that could make them both cleaner and safer, SUVs and other light trucks are still held to low environmental standards, roll over more than cars and pose greater danger to other vehicles than cars do.

The world's leading climate scientists have warned that there is now 30 percent more carbon dioxide—the primary global-warming gas—in the atmosphere than a century ago. The burning of fossil fuels is the primary source of this CO_2

pollution. Over the same period of time, the average surface temperature of the earth has risen more than 1 degree Fahrenheit.

Due to these changes, we are already seeing signs of global warming. The 1990s was the hottest decade on record and the 11 hottest years on record have all occurred in the past 13 years.

SUV Wastefulness Cancels Other Gains

One SUV like the Explorer . . . could wipe out energy conservation gains being made in other sectors of the economy. Take, for example, efficiency in building lighting, then being pushed by EPA [Environmental Protection Agency] in a voluntary 1992 business program called Green Lights, aimed also at reducing greenhouse gases.

American Express joined the program and began installing new energy efficient lighting in its offices. At the company's fifty-one-story office building in Manhattan, American Express saved up to 40 percent on electricity bills while cutting carbon emissions. Together with offices in five other cities, American Express cut annual CO_2 emissions by 3,000 metric tons. Yet on the national ledger of carbon give and take, this impressive savings by American Express was wiped out by the CO_2 emitted by 700 Ford Explorers—less than one day's production of that model.

Jack Doyle, *Taken for a Ride*, 2000.

Extreme drought conditions and changing rainfall patterns have occurred across the country, setting the stage for wildfires, which decimated areas from Florida to California. Record heat waves have killed hundreds in Chicago and infectious-disease outbreaks linked to global warming have sickened or killed hundreds from Texas to New York, shut down Disney World and re-introduced Americans to dengue fever, malaria and encephalitis. Sea levels have risen between four and 10 inches and glacial ice is rapidly retreating on five continents.

The world's leading scientists warn that over the 21st century, CO_2 levels are expected to double, raising sea levels two feet or more, worsening smog and leaving our children to cope with a more hostile climate.

America's cars and light trucks alone produce nearly 20

percent of U.S. CO_2 pollution. That's more than all but four countries worldwide! And transportation is the fastest-growing sector of global-warming pollution in the nation. Popular light trucks pump out 237 million tons of global-warming pollution into our atmosphere each year. That's because every gallon of gas burned emits 28 pounds of CO_2 into the atmosphere.

SUVs Emit More Air Pollution than Cars

Nearly 117 million Americans live in areas where the air is unhealthy to breathe, according to the American Lung Association. Light trucks, which can spew up to three times more smog-forming pollution than cars, magnify this growing health threat. The increased air pollution can lead to more asthma, bronchitis and other health problems.

U.S. autos emit more CO_2 than all but four countries.
Top 5 Global-Warming Polluters:
1. U.S.
2. China
3. Russia
4. Japan
5. U.S. autos

Air pollution is not exclusively an urban problem. National parks from Maine's Acadia to Virginia's Shenandoah and North Carolina's Great Smokey Mountains all have severe air-pollution problems that match major metropolitan areas. Pollution monitors are now installed at some trailheads in Mt. Rainier National Park to warn hikers when smog reaches unsafe levels.

The U.S. Environmental Protection Agency adopted new "Tier 2" tailpipe pollution standards in 1999 to cut smog (but not CO_2) from cars and SUVs. However, these rules will not go into effect until 2004 and the auto industry has until 2009 to clean up its largest SUVs.

SUVs Increase Our Oil Addiction, Threaten Our Wilderness and Coasts

A hidden cost of SUVs is the price we pay with our natural resources. To keep these gas guzzlers running, oil companies seek to drill in new areas—including some of our nation's most sensitive wilderness habitats. As the number of gas guzzlers on the road grows, so does the pressure to drill in Alaska's Arctic National Wildlife Refuge—one of the last remaining pristine ecosystems. Fragile coastlines in California and Florida, and lands surrounding Yellowstone National Park, are also targets for drilling.

The Exxon *Valdez* disaster serves as a powerful reminder that transporting oil also threatens our environment. Smaller spills and leaks occur daily, putting waterways and wildlife at risk.

Worsening Our Energy Security

Every day America consumes 18 million barrels of oil. We import nearly half of this oil (the same amount guzzled by cars and light trucks) from politically volatile regions. Our oil imports add $50 billion to the U.S. trade deficit annually. Due to the increasing number of gas-guzzling vehicles, America is more dependent on foreign oil now than we were at the height of the 1973 energy crisis.

Congress passed the Corporate Average Fuel Economy (CAFE) standards in 1975 to reduce our dangerous oil dependence. This doubled the fuel economy of America's vehicle fleet, saving 3 million barrels of oil per day. However, the oil savings from CAFE standards are being eroded by people driving farther and the rising proportion of inefficient SUVs and other light trucks. In fact, the average fuel economy of new vehicles has sunk to the lowest level since 1980. Raising the CAFE standard for light trucks to equal that of cars (27.5 mpg) would save 1 million barrels of oil per day. We can do even better. Raising the average for cars to 45 mpg and light trucks to 34 mpg would save 3 million barrels of oil per day.

Available technology and higher mileage standards could make the popular Ford Explorer a 34.1 mpg vehicle, rather than a 19.3 mpg guzzler, without compromising performance or safety. This "improved" Explorer could emit 43 percent less global-warming pollution and 76 percent less smog-forming pollution and cost only $935 more. Consumers would save several times this at the gas pump over the life of the vehicle.

Industry Foot-Dragging and Excuses

History shows that automakers won't improve the environmental performance of their products unless they are required to put technology to work. Raising CAFE standards is the key to cleaning up SUVs and other light trucks.

In 1974, a Ford official testified before Congress that CAFE standards would "result in a Ford product line consisting of either all sub-Pinto-sized vehicles or some mix of vehicles ranging from a sub-sub-compact to perhaps a Maverick." Today, automakers use similar arguments against improving CAFE standards for SUVs. The claim wasn't true then; it isn't true today. Eighty-six percent of the fuel-economy improvements for cars have resulted from improved technologies such as more efficient engines and transmissions and better aerodynamics.

In July 2000, Ford promised to use technology that will improve its SUVs' fuel economy by 25 percent over five years. General Motors pledged to exceed Ford's light-truck fuel economy. Keeping these promises will begin the process of cleaning up SUVs.

But Detroit continues to fight higher CAFE standards for light trucks and cars, which would guarantee these and other improvements. The auto industry has taken its fight to Congress, getting its friends to fight legislation that would increase fuel economy. Beginning in 1995, Congress froze CAFE standards at levels set decades ago.

Americans Deserve Vehicles That Are Both Safe and Clean

Detroit opposes CAFE standards, claiming that they cannot make a safe, clean SUV. Contrary to the auto industry's arguments, CAFE standards don't dictate automobile size or safety. Design, not weight, is the key to both safety and fuel economy. Engineering and safety features like airbags and crush-resistant roofs can ensure that vehicles absorb crash forces so occupants don't. Crash-test results show that automakers are making safe and unsafe cars of all sizes. In a standard head-on crash test into a wall, occupants of a 1997 Ford Expedition faced greater risk of injury or death than occupants of a 1997 Saturn subcompact. This is because the

Saturn has crashworthiness designed into it and the Expedition does not.

The same industry claimed the original CAFE law was a threat to highway safety, battled automotive safety improvements from seatbelts to airbags and continues to fight a rollover standard. The fact is that since 1975 CAFE standards doubled fuel economy and the rate of highway fatalities fell by 50 percent.

The SUV Safety Story: Rollovers and Dangers to Others on the Road

Here's what the *New York Times* said about SUV safety (July 15, 1999): "Because it is taller, heavier and more rigid, an SUV or a pickup is more than twice as likely as a car to kill the driver of the other vehicle in a collision. Yet partly because these so-called light trucks roll over so often, their occupants have roughly the same chance as car occupants of dying in a crash."

SUVs give a false impression of safety. With their height and comparatively narrow tire-track width, SUVs handle and maneuver much less effectively than cars. Emergency swerves to avoid a crash can themselves lead to rollover accidents in SUVs, which are four times more likely to roll over in an accident. Rollovers account for 62 percent of SUV deaths but only 22 percent in cars. Yet automakers continue to fight new standards that would protect occupants in rollover accidents.

Because SUVs are built on high, stiff frames, their bumpers ride above the occupant-protecting frame of cars. When an SUV and a car collide, this height difference, combined with the stiff battering-ram frame and greater mass, create a lethal weapon.

According to a government study, in 1996 "at least 2,000 car occupants would not have been killed, had their cars collided with other cars instead of trucks of the same weight." And SUVs are also more deadly to pedestrians, bicyclists and motorcyclists than cars, in part because existing braking standards for SUVs are weaker than for cars.

The Biggest Single Step to Curb Global Warming

Beginning in 1995, friends of the auto industry in Congress attacked CAFE standards with an anti-environmental "rider" in the Department of Transportation's funding bill. The rider forbids the administration from setting new CAFE standards. While technology exists to safely improve fuel economy and protect our environment, the CAFE-freeze rider allows the auto industry to remain stuck in reverse.

It is time for action. Please urge your public officials to support cleaning up our cars and light trucks. Ask them to help take the first step of closing the loophole that allows SUVs and other light trucks to guzzle more gas than cars. Tell them our children have a right to a safe and healthy environment. It's time to take the biggest single step to curb global warming.

"It's not all those capitalists driving those sinister SUVs, but the irascible old Sun causing this whole mess."

Sport Utility Vehicles Do Not Contribute to Global Warming

Sal Rosken

In the following viewpoint Sal Rosken argues that efforts to blame sport utility vehicles (SUVs) for global warming are driven more by politics than by science. Drawing on the idea that environmentalists are against industrialization and capitalism, Rosken contends that environmentalists target SUVs as a symbolic step toward returning humans to a preindustrial way of life. Their reasoning is faulty, Rosken argues, because it is solar activity, not human industrial activity, that causes global warming. Rosken is a private investor in New York and a frequent contributor to the *Partial Observer*, a Web site that publishes opinion pieces from a variety of perspectives.

As you read, consider the following questions:

1. According to Rosken, are human beings capable of changing the global climate?
2. How does Rosken perceive the U.S. media in terms of their coverage of environmental issues?
3. According to the viewpoint, how does the BBC article argue against SUVs and industrial greenhouse emissions causing temperature increases?

Global warming is causing the end of civilization as we know it. The polar ice caps, once pristine and frozen in their majesty, are melting with an alarming rapidity. The rapacious oceans are rising daily; and within one hundred years major coastal cities around the world will sink ignominiously beneath the waves. Typhoons, Hurricanes, Monsoons and Tornadoes, whipped to a Coriolisian frenzy by the warmer atmosphere, will ravage the land; while drought will increasingly decimate the crops we depend upon, causing famine and widespread starvation. Forest fires will burn uncontrollably throughout the parched land, destroying millions of acres of primitive woodland. Jungles and rain forests, the repositories of the pharmaceutical secrets of the world, will disappear with a stunning alacrity. Thousands of animal species in all zoological phyla, ranging from polar bears to the tiniest exotic finches, will die off due to the loss of their natural habitats, and become extinct. Mankind, left alone in a blasted landscape, will be reduced to a brutish Darwinian existence before he succumbs finally to the diseases that will spread uncontrollably through a diminished and wretched population.

And all of this will occur, most assuredly, because you drive a Sport Utility Vehicle (SUV).

Faith, Not Science

At least, that is the apocalyptic prophecy being served up by the Fire and Brimstone Environmental Lobbyists and their Media lackeys, who are now experimenting with Religion (What Would Jesus Drive) and Geopolitics (SUVs support Terrorism) in their bid to save us from ourselves by eradicating first SUVs, then the internal combustion engine, and ultimately all industrial expansion.

As is the case with all fundamentalist believers and soothsayers there is not an inkling of doubt among the faithful in the Environmentalist's ranks. Their cause is just. Only belief and faith are necessary. It is an article of faith, not of science, that global climate change resulting from human industrial activity will be the cause of the impending doom. Verifiable and replicative, scientific proof, the sort which most of the same environmental activists require pharmaceutical and agricultural companies to provide to the Food and Drug Administration (FDA) before marketing medicines and genetically modified foods, does not seem to enter into the environmentalist's calculus when proscribing human activities which have been adjudged, by their prescient minds, as contributing to global warming.

Most scientific studies and measurements do suggest something is happening with the climate, but if the environmental lobbyists, before launching anti–greenhouse gas and anti-SUV marketing campaigns, were held to the same standard of proof determining causality that the FDA requires of corporations marketing drugs, there would be little of the hysteria now pervading the media.

The real issue that needs examination and debate is not whether global warming is or is not occurring; it may very well be. We simply do not know, and it cannot be determined with certainty, given the state of our current scientific knowledge and measurement techniques.

The truly salient issue that begs to be exposed is the overwhelming hubris exhibited by the environmental lobbyists in believing humans can actually influence and control the global climate. This, combined with the habitual use of some very flawed science, by politically motivated amateurs determined to "prove" global warming is the direct result of human industrial activity, has so dominated and cozened the popular Media, that any rational discussion of scientific fact has become virtually impossible.

Cosmic Rays

Consider an article by Alex Kirby entitled "Cosmic Rays linked to Clouds" which appeared in the *BBC* [British Broadcasting Corporation] *On Line News* last October; and which received virtually no notice in the Environmentalist biased US media.

"German scientists" the BBC reported, "have found a significant piece of evidence linking cosmic rays to climate change. They have detected charged particle clusters in the lower atmosphere that were probably caused by the space radiation. They say the clusters can lead to the condensed nuclei which form into dense clouds."

The scientific study, performed under the auspices of the Max Planck Institute of Nuclear Physics in Heidelberg, [Germany] makes the case, as reported by the BBC, that Solar generated cosmic rays produce particle clusters in the atmosphere, which then form dense clouds. These clouds then act to cool and warm the atmosphere by absorbing and reflecting infrared, solar and terrestrial radiation. An increase or decrease in Solar activity, such as the recently noted increase in Sun Spots and Solar Flares, would therefore have a much more direct effect on the warming or cooling of the atmosphere than previously thought.

Wright. © 2003 by *The Detroit News*. Reproduced by permission.

"Clouds" the BBC article reports, "play a major, but as yet not fully understood, role in the dynamics of the climate, with some types acting to cool the planet and others warming it up. The amount of cosmic rays reaching Earth is largely controlled by the Sun, and many solar scientists believe the star's indirect influence on Earth's global climate has been underestimated. Some think a significant part of the global warming recorded in [the] 20th Century may in fact have its origin in changes in solar activity—not just in the increase in fossil-fuel-produced greenhouse gases."

You would think that this would have been considered big news. Hey, you might conclude, there is a possibility, an outside chance at least, that it's not all those capitalists driving those sinister SUVs, but the irascible old Sun causing this whole mess. First, interference with radio signals, then skin cancer, and now global warming. The Sun is warming the Earth. Who would have thought?

Evidence Ignored

But the article received scant notice, nary a mention in the US media. It would be asking too much of those, so invested in blaming greenhouse gases, to admit that perhaps they weren't right after all. And the popular media needs a protagonist (the crusading environmentalists) and an antagonist (the profiteering industrialists), locked in a death struggle (conflict), to make a compelling human-interest story of good versus evil. And let's not even mention the Geopolitical impact this inopportune information may have on the sacrosanct Kyoto Treaty [regulating greenhouse gas emissions].

"Depending on whether and how cloud cover changes," the BBC article continues, "the cloud feedback could almost halve or almost double the warming. Many scientists agree that the Earth's surface appears to be warming, while low atmosphere temperatures remain unchanged. Research published [in August 2002] suggested the rays might cause changes in cloud cover, which could explain the temperature conundrum. The discrepancy in temperatures has led some scientists to argue that the case for human-induced climate change is weak, because our influence should presumably show a uniform temperature rise from the surface up through the atmosphere."

In short, if greenhouse gases produced by human industrial activity were causing temperature increases consistent with global warming, the scientific evidence gathered thus far would be much different.

Flawed Models

This scientific study, however, is not the only evidence pointing to an overzealous, politically motivated attribution of global warming to human industrial activity. Other scientists have noted that most of the scientific equipment used to measure temperatures in the studies claiming to prove the existence of global warming have been located near large cities and are only measuring local increases in temperatures at the earth's surface resulting from industrial expansion within those cities. This is a far cry, and a huge difference, from proving scientifically that the global atmosphere is warming.

Other scientists have noted that the variables and dynamics involved in global climate changes are so complex and diverse that the ability to model them is far beyond the capability of even the fastest supercomputers; in fact, these same scientists point out, the computer models that are being used to argue the case for global warming are filled with so many assumptions and conjectures, which are necessitated by the enormous lack of scientific knowledge on just how global climate really works, that any of the models' results are suspect at best, and meaningless at worst.

That increases in temperatures at certain points on the surface of the Earth are occurring is not in much doubt; what is in great doubt, however, are the actual causes of this warming and whether this constitutes a global warming which will result in the apocalyptic visions being called up by the environmental lobbyists to scare us back into a Ludditian and Agrarian existence dependent on Pre-Industrial Revolution Cottage Industries producing goods affordable by only the rich.

The Environmental Groups and Media types who champion their cause have taken it as an article of faith, not science, that human industrial activity is the cause of a potentially disastrous climate change. But if one holds that human activity in the form of industrial expansion is the cause of this most recent spate of global warming, one then has an obligation and duty to explain scientifically what caused the expansion of the glaciers during the last Ice Age and their subsequent retreat during the last global warming. There were no greenhouse gases then, no industrial expansion then, and most certainly no SUVs being driven by capitalist industrialists advocating globalization.

Can it be possible that, just maybe, mankind is not actually in control, and is simply along for the ride?

"Past and recent climate warming can be explained by changes in solar activity. And the data exist to support it."

Solar Activity Causes Global Warming

Ian Clark

Recent analysis of satellite data has provided important new ways of understanding solar activity, reports Ian Clark in the following viewpoint. Addressing fellow Canadians, Clark argues that although members of the government believe that following the recommendations of the international Kyoto Protocol to reduce greenhouse gas emissions will slow down global warming, the Protocol ignores the true cause of global climate change—the sun. When the sun radiates more energy, the Earth experiences global warming, he maintains. Clark is a professor of hydrogeology and paleoclimatology at the University of Ottawa, and is an expert on Arctic geology and climate change.

As you read, consider the following questions:

1. Why, in Clark's opinion, do some people want to believe that humans are causing global warming?
2. How consistent, according to the author, is the supposed correlation between CO_2 levels and temperature?
3. How do storms on the sun's surface affect Earth's atmosphere, as described by the author?

[T]he] Kyoto [climate treaty] and climate change have at last become election issues. And why not? Many people in the more wealthy parts of the world consider climate warming our greatest environmental threat, with new extremes in weather and damage to fragile ecosystems wrought by our CO_2 emissions. [Canada's] Environment Minister tells us that the science of Kyoto is "solid" and "settled," and that we must accept to spend billions of dollars on attempts to stop global climate change. Most of us endorse policies that improve air quality. We also embrace technologies that improve fuel efficiencies. However, the Kyoto Protocol is being sold, not for these reasonable objectives, but on the pretence that we can thwart an impending climate disaster. Nothing could be further from the truth.

CO_2's skyward trajectory during the industrial era does indeed appear alarming. Moreover, this rise has occurred during a period of global warming that has delivered us from four cold centuries known as the Little Ice Age. Both temperature and CO_2 seem to ascend in unison like the twin contrails of the Space Shuttle, leading the public, and even many scientists, to conclude that increasing CO_2 is driving temperatures higher.

Yet, too few observers have considered the possibility that we have the science backwards—that temperature rise is driven by factors unrelated to human activity, and that CO_2 is following in the wake. Blaming ourselves as the Machiavellian hand wreaking climate disaster satisfies a sense of collective guilt, and also engenders the anthropocentric view that humans are so powerful that our actions are a major global climate determinant. The corollary to this has even greater appeal—all we need to do is tweak CO_2 emissions and we can turn it around and "stop climate change."

Humans Cannot Affect Global Climate

The problem with this hypothesis is that it is undoubtedly wrong—we haven't affected global climate, never have and never could. Furthermore, there is no chance that we will effect measurable climate changes with Kyoto or any other accord, or with technologies we can deploy in the foreseeable future.

Many scientists know this and some are even brave enough to say so publicly. Other scientists recognize that the politically correct view of human-caused climate change is largely unfounded but remain loyal to the cause because this is their source of research funding. Others stay quiet because they believe that cutting greenhouse gas emissions will have the side benefit of reducing air pollution (it may or may not, depending on the application). Or because they believe that reducing resource consumption is generally good for our moral well-being.

However, there are many enormously expensive and environmentally dangerous initiatives being promoted to reduce CO_2 emissions in the name of Kyoto: the twisted logic of subsidizing ethanol production (with collateral environmental damage from pesticides and fertilizers) and "sequestering" power plant CO_2 emissions deep underground are just two of them. And the trading of green credits [the buying and selling of permission to emit greenhouse gases] will most certainly benefit lawyers and corporations' bottom lines, but not the environment.

To appreciate the mistake that is Kyoto, one must first understand what really drives climate.

Carbon Dioxide Has Little Effect on Climate

Weighing in at more than 10,000 parts per million and taking gold, silver and bronze medals as the principal greenhouse gas in our atmosphere, is naturally occurring water vapour, the stuff that gives us clouds, rain and snow. Were it not for water vapour, Earth's temperature would be about 30 degrees colder than it is today. At 360 parts per million, CO_2 is only a very minor player in the greenhouse gas Olympics. So increasing its concentration by 32%, as has happened since the beginning of the industrial era, or even doubling it by the year 2100 (a highly unlikely proposition) will do little to raise temperatures. In fact, the correlation between CO_2 levels and temperature rise over the past century is actually quite poor, as it fails to capture the distinctive cooling trend of the 1960s and '70s when greenhouse gases were increasing at the highest rate in recent history.

But what about ice core studies that Kyoto supporters cite

as "proof" that CO_2 rise directly results in temperature increase over long time periods? Studies by paleo-climate researchers reveal that, while CO_2 and temperature do indeed rise and fall in close unison over much of the record, temperature increases actually preceded CO_2 rise by as much as 800 years or more.

So where do the dire predictions of increases of three to four degrees come from?

Computers are used to simulate climate and predict warming by increased CO_2, based on the fundamental laws of physics. However, the amount of warming they determine from predicted CO_2 rises doesn't warm the simulated atmosphere much at all. They predict measurable warming only by presuming that an increase in CO_2 will trigger a much greater increase in water vapour, and that the water vapour will raise global temperatures. While this implicates CO_2 as a prominent indirect climate driver, it remains a theoretical and untested hypothesis. Lacking confidence in the veracity of the CO_2-climate link, it seems absurd to spend billions of dollars on a scheme to slightly reduce the rate of CO_2 increase in the hopes that it will ameliorate global temperature rise.

So, if not increased atmospheric CO_2, what is driving climate warming?

Solar Activity Controls Climate

Not so surprisingly, it's the sun. Scientists have discovered good correlations between trends in the output of the sun and temperature, measured using proxy data from climate indicators such as tree rings and ice cores. These data are not theoretical. They are real climate records that span many time scales. And all point to solar variation as being the primary driver of climate change. Like CO_2, they fit with warming in the first half of the 20th century. However, unlike CO_2, they trace the cooling trend of the 1960s and 1970s, and even the apparent warming of the past two decades. There is even a strong correlation between solar activity, temperature and cloudiness—the most direct and telling line of evidence for a heliocentric [sun-determined] climate.

As the source of most of our planet's energy, it is astounding that more scientists did not suspect the sun to be the driver of today's global warming. We were clearly misled by the apparent temperature-CO_2 correlation as well as our lack of appreciation of the variable nature of our home star. Until recent satellite observations showed variations in radiant output from the sun, its output was commonly referred to in textbooks as "the solar constant." We know now that it is anything but steady and that the sun is more active today than it has been in centuries. Evidence for this is found in the number of sunspots, a measure of solar activity and a record carefully established since the 1600s when Galileo invented the telescope.

The Variable Sun

Depending on whether the nucleus of the Sun is closer or farther removed from the center of mass of the solar system, and depending on the Sun's position in its oscillation around that center of mass, solar activity ranges from being virtually absent to being very pronounced. During periods of high solar activity, the energy radiated by the Sun increases, and therefore the Earth receives more radiation from the Sun and heats up. Moreover, solar activities also interfere with the amount of cosmic radiation that reaches the atmosphere of the Earth. Then there will be also a corresponding reduction in cloud formation and therefore less precipitation. When the Sun has a long interval of relatively large energy output, the Earth experiences global warming. When the energy output by the Sun is low for an extended interval, the Earth cools off. If such a quiet interval lasts for a very long time, the Earth experiences an ice age.

Bruderheim Rea, "Global Warming Explained," www.fathersforlife.org, September 26, 2002.

However, linked with increased solar activity is an effect that was largely unknown until recently. Two decades of satellite data have revealed that when the sun is more active, storms on its surface, manifested by sunspots, are accompanied by strong increases in "solar wind," a continuous stream of charged particles ejected from the outermost layer of the solar atmosphere into space. An increase in solar wind acts to deflect away from the Earth an even more energetic form of radiation that is continuously streaming into our solar system from the galaxy. Referred to as "galactic cosmic rays"

(GCR), these high-energy particles cause an electric charge to build up on dust and other small particles in our atmosphere, which in turn causes them to attract water molecules and so form clouds. Of course, clouds, particularly high clouds, reflect a lot of incoming sunlight back into space, which acts to cool the planet. Not surprisingly, there is a strong correlation between temperature and the measured index of cloudiness.

So the total effect of the sun appears to be more significant than previously thought. When the sun is brighter, not only do we experience more direct heating, but the more intense solar wind "blows" away incoming GCR which in turn warms the planet through a reduction in cloud cover. Thus, past and recent climate warming can be explained by changes in solar activity. And the data exist to support it.

The Example of Copernicus

Which brings us to Nicholas Copernicus. The timid Canon of Warmi, Poland, spent much of his career deconvolving [disproving] the Earth-centered universe theory, with its wild gyrations in the solar system invented by clergy scientists to account for the observed motions of the planets. Copernicus discovered a much simpler heliocentric universe where the celestial bodies orbited the sun, obeying the established laws of physics.

What was his secret? He looked for a solution to explain what he saw, unencumbered by the Church's constraint that if God created the Earth, it must be at the centre of the universe. Intimidated by the overpowering forces of political correctness, Copernicus delayed publishing his magnificent work until the very end of his life and received a copy of the printed book for the first time on his deathbed.

In the intended preface to his book, Copernicus wrote: "Perhaps there will be babblers who, although completely ignorant of mathematics, nevertheless take it upon themselves to pass judgment on mathematical questions and, badly distorting some passages to Scripture to their purpose, will dare to find fault with my undertaking and censure it. I disregard them even to the extent as despising their criticism as unfounded."

Much like Copernicus, the many climate experts who have moved away from the clergy science of Kyoto seek with an open mind to understand the real, testable and observable mechanics of climate. These scientists are the vanguard of a modern Copernican revolution that should be encouraged by all thinking Canadians.

"Evidence indicates that the cause of oceans heating is a hot spot rotating in the earth's core."

Radiation from the Earth's Core Causes Global Warming

Gary Novak

Those who blame carbon dioxide for global warming are mistaken, argues Gary Novak in the following viewpoint. He contends that the atmosphere is warming because the oceans are heating up, and that they in turn are heated by a hot spot in the Earth's core. Only this, he claims, could account for the cyclical nature of recurring warm spells and ice ages. Novak is an independent biologist and moral philosopher. He maintains a Web site titled *Science Criticism*, which explores global warming, ice ages, the Earth's core, and other issues.

As you read, consider the following questions:

1. As reported by the author, what percentage of the Earth's atmosphere is made up of carbon dioxide?
2. According to the viewpoint, what processes work to make greenhouse gases hold heat on the planet?
3. How do we know that the Earth's core is in motion, as explained by Novak?

Do you realize how stupid people look when they say 0.04% of the atmosphere (CO_2) is causing global warming while not knowing everything else in the atmosphere is a greenhouse gas also? It's like saying ants on the road determine gas mileage.

Oceans Heating Is the Cause of Global Warming

There is a major factor being overlooked in the claim that carbon dioxide is the cause of global warming. Everything in the atmosphere is a greenhouse gas, while only a miniscule part is being referred to as greenhouse gasses. Carbon dioxide is only 0.04% of the atmosphere.

The real greenhouse gasses include nitrogen 78%, oxygen 20% and water vapor 0–3%. They absorb and reemit infrared radiation just like CO_2 does, and they conduct and convect heat which the sun produces. Nitrogen and oxygen do not absorb radiation as effectively as CO_2, but they make up 2,500 times as much of the atmosphere. Water vapor absorbs in a comparable way to CO_2, and there is up to 100 times as much of it in the atmosphere. Water vapor varies greatly, while CO_2 changes slightly.

An important fact that is not being mentioned is that absorption of radiation in the atmosphere is not the only factor creating the greenhouse effect. Conduction and convection also add heat, and they are much more significant than radiation. Instead of these factors being considered, the entire greenhouse effect is being attributed to radiation absorbed by the micro components, as on the web site of the Union of Concerned Scientists.

There, the greenhouse effect is said to increase the temperature of the earth by 59°F. But since only CO_2 and the micro components are mentioned, the impression is that they create the entire greenhouse effect. No way, shape or form does 0.04% of the atmosphere do all of that. The nitrogen, oxygen and water vapor are responsible for about 58.98 of those 59 degrees.

The Role of Conduction and Convection

The very important effect of holding heat on the planet through greenhouse gasses is due almost entirely to conduction and convection, not the radiation effect attributed to CO_2 and the micro components. Conduction and convection work like this: The sun's heat strikes the surface of the earth as radiation and is converted into heat. This heat is in the soil, rocks, plants, water, etc. Then air sweeps over the surface and picks up the heat through conduction and convection, which heats the air.

Earth as a Nuclear Reactor

Consequences of global warming are far more serious than previously imagined. The REAL danger for our entire civilization comes not from slow climate changes, but from overheating of the planetary interior.

Life on Earth is possible only because of the efficient cooling of the planetary interior—a process that is limited primarily by the atmosphere. This cooling is responsible for a thermal balance between the heat from the core reactor, the heat from the Sun and the radiation of heat into space, so that the average temperature on Earth's surface is about 13 degrees Celsius. . . .

It is common knowledge (experiencing seasons) that solar heat is the dominant factor that determines temperatures on the surface of Earth. Under the polar ice, however, the contribution of solar heat is minimal and this is where the increasing contribution of the heat from the planetary interior can be seen best. Rising polar ocean temperatures and melting polar ice caps should therefore be the first symptoms of overheating of the inner core reactor.

While politicians and businessmen debate the need for reducing greenhouse emissions and take pride to evade accepting any responsibility, the process of overheating the inner core reactor has already begun—polar oceans have become warmer and polar caps have begun to melt. Do we have enough imagination, intelligence and integrity to comprehend the danger before the situation becomes irreversible? There will be NO SECOND CHANCE.

Tom J. Chalko, *Natural University Journal of Discovery*, October 30, 2004.

Conduction means a heated molecule bumps into another molecule and causes it to pick up the heat as vibratory motion. Then the heated molecule is moved out of the way through convection, so another molecule can be heated in the same way. This is how the atmosphere is heated. Any heat added by radiation striking CO_2 is only a trace amount.

Global warming is observed as weather changes including ice sheets melting, which are certainly real effects. But such effects are not being caused by CO_2 in the air. They are caused by oceans warming plus black soot accumulating on the ice.

The Earth's Core

The uniform assumption has been that there could be no other cause of global warming than CO_2 and other micro components of the atmosphere. That assumption is totally absurd. Evidence indicates that the cause of oceans heating is a hot spot rotating in the earth's core. Ice age cycles point to this, because they have been cycling at exactly 100 thousand year intervals for the past million years. Environmental effects would be much more random. A rotating mass in the earth's core would be cyclic.

The fact that the magnetic north pole is constantly moving shows that the earth's core is heterogeneous and in motion. Fluids always are in motion due to convection, and many other forces could act upon the earth's core.

Convecting fluids are never uniform in temperature. The temperature of air in a still room varies by several degrees due to convectional currents. Similarly, variations in the temperature of the earth's core should be expected due to convection and nonuniformity of the earth's surface, where loss of heat cools the core.

The earth's core is constantly cooling, resulting in an increasingly thick mantle. A billion years ago, the earth's crust was so thin that collisions of tectonic plates did not create mountains. The evolution of mountains is an indication of the rate of cooling of the earth's core.

A New Ice Age?

Oceans heating may, or may not, indicate another ice age beginning. Mini ice ages do occur. But another ice age is due to occur at this time based upon the cycling of previous ice ages. If an ice age is beginning, how will it occur?

First, heating of the oceans will cause increased precipitation everywhere. There is evidence of slight increases in precipitation in recent years. Lake Michigan has been rising and flooding Chicago; and to control it, another canal was built around Niagara Falls during the early nineties.

After precipitation increases to a much higher level, and there is much more snowfall in northern areas, a trigger mechanism starts a precipitous drop in temperature. The most likely trigger would be a volcano which clouds the sky and prevents snow from melting. The unmelted snow would reflect away the sun's heat triggering a rapid cool-down of the planet.

It is conceivable that no trigger mechanism would be needed to start an ice age, if high levels of precipitation cause more snow to accumulate than can melt. This could be a gradual process, as more and more snow accumulates each year.

For a time scale, it would probably take at least 50 years, and more likely 100–200 years, for rainfall to increase enough to start the reversal, if the present global warming is the start of another ice age.

Periodical Bibliography

The following articles have been selected to supplement the diverse views presented in this chapter.

Gerry Byrne	"Sun Fuels Debate on Climate Change," *New Scientist*, April 12, 2003.
John Carey	"Global Warming," *Business Week*, August 16, 2004.
Thomas J. Crowley	"Causes of Climate Change over the Past 1,000 Years," *Science*, July 14, 2000.
Environment	"Global Warming: Sun Takes Some Heat," October 2004.
Mark Z. Jacobson	"The Short-Term Cooling but Long-Term Global Warming Due to Biomass Burning," *Journal of Climate*, August 1, 2004.
Eugenia Kalnay and Ming Cai	"Impact of Urbanization and Land-Use on Climate," *Nature*, May 29, 2003.
Marianne Lavelle	"A Shift in the Wind on Global Warming," *U.S. News & World Report*, March 19, 2001.
Kim Y. Masibay	"Does My Gas Cause Global Warming? Belches and Flatulence Are Harmless, Right? Wrong! When Cattle and Sheep Burp and Pass Gas, the Entire Planet Reels," *Science World*, January 21, 2002.
Fred Pearce	"Earth Heats Up as the Smog Clears," *New Scientist*, May 14, 2005.
Curtis Runyan	"Ocean Warming Studies Bolster Evidence of Human Hand in Climate Change," *World Watch*, July/August 2001.
Sarah Simpson	"Methane Fever: An Undersea Methane Explosion May Have Driven the Most Rapid Warming Episode of the Past 90 Million Years," *Scientific American*, February 2000.
Kevin E. Trenberth	"Stronger Evidence of Human Influences on Climate: The 2001 IPCC Assessment," *Environment*, May 2001.
Francis W. Zwiers and Andrew J. Weaver	"The Causes of 20th Century Warming," *Science*, December 15, 2000.

CHAPTER 3

What Will Be the Effects of Global Warming?

Chapter Preface

While American media largely ignore the technical aspects of global warming, the debate over possible dangers has entered the popular imagination. An exaggerated view of how quickly climate change could happen was depicted in a recent disaster movie, *The Day After Tomorrow* (2004). In the film, a lonely scientist warns about the dangers of global warming but is ignored. In spectacular fashion, most of the Northern Hemisphere is destroyed in just a few days by tornadoes, blizzards, floods, and a new ice age. Though policy makers express regret at the destruction, a character scolds, "You didn't want to listen to the science when it could have made a difference." In contrast, the writer Michael Crichton presents a world under the influence of global warming alarmists in his novel *State of Fear* (2004). The story involves environmental terrorists determined to destroy an ice shelf in order to persuade more people of the threat of global warming. In his preface Crichton discredits the global warming alarmists and their "near-hysterical preoccupation with safety that's at best a waste of resources and a crimp on the human spirit, and at worst an invitation to totalitarianism."

While scientific disagreement is usually much less dramatic than the dialogue in a film or novel, something approaching this level of passion colors the debate over how serious the effects of global warming, if it exists, might be if steps are not taken to slow or stop it. Perhaps because the environmental, economic, and political stakes are so high, this debate has driven its participants to strong and vivid language.

Scientists who believe that global warming poses a serious threat have warned of dire effects. Left unchecked, they argue, global warming could lead to devastating flooding at the coasts due to rising sea levels, and drought and famine in the interior lands because of decreased precipitation. Diseases and pests that have been contained to certain areas by freezing temperatures in winter could enlarge their habitats and find millions of new victims. Hans Blix, chief weapons inspector for the United Nations, said in 2003, "I'm more worried about global warming than I am of any major military conflict."

Other scientists and writers dismiss these claims as alarmist. They explain that global warming might offer benefits that outweigh any potential harm, including increased crop production due to longer growing seasons, fewer deaths due to cold, and fewer icy roads. The people who are predicting death and destruction, they argue, are not trying to save the Earth. Instead, they contend, the alarmists are trying to keep contributions flowing into their environmental organizations, or, as writer Tom DeWeese explains it, to lessen the emissions of American factories in order to bring about "redistribution of wealth from the rich, developed nations to jealous dictatorships who refuse to allow their citizens to gain their own wealth through free markets."

The authors in the following chapter are scientists and journalists, not fiction writers. But they bring passion to their examinations of the effects of global warming.

| *"Palmer Station [in Antarctica] . . . may be the most warmed-up place on the planet."*

Global Warming Is Causing the Polar Ice Caps to Melt

Charles W. Petit

According to Charles W. Petit in the following viewpoint, global warming is heating up the Antarctic, leading to serious environmental disruption. As the air has heated up, the ice shelf has begun breaking apart, he argues. As a result, krill, the young of which shelter under the ice shelf, are dying off. Because krill constitute the primary food source for penguins, which are in turn eaten by other arctic animals, the demise of these creatures could have catastrophic results on arctic ecology, according to Petit. Charles W. Petit writes for *U.S. News & World Report.*

As you read, consider the following questions:

1. By how much have temperatures increased on the Antarctic Peninsula, according to Petit?
2. As reported by the author, how many more Adelie penguins nested by Palmer Station twenty-five years ago?
3. What anecdote about Adelie penguins does the author relate to show how inflexible they are?

One doesn't need a Ph.D. to see that things are changing fast around here. "That's Dead Seal Point up there," says Ross Hein, 27, director of boating operations at this remote American research base. On a sunny January day—midsummer in Antarctica—he points the Zodiac inflated motorboat toward a low, rocky islet a mile or so east of the base. The tough, flexible bow bumps slowly through a shoal of ice chunks—some the size of golf balls, others as big as a refrigerator—shoved near shore by the wind and current. The hard ice gives the boat a ride like an old truck on a bad road. It leads into a startlingly beautiful passage several hundred yards long and 50 yards wide. "[In 1998]," Hein marvels, "this wasn't even here."

Dead Seal Point

The point is that Dead Seal Point has no point, for we clearly are passing behind an island. To the right is a long wall of extravagantly fractured ice high as a 10-story building. It is the leading edge of Marr Ice Piedmont, a glacial cap that reaches a depth of 2,000 feet on 38-mile-long Anvers Island, Palmer's home 120 miles outside the Antarctic Circle. Hein, to minimize hazards from falling ice, keeps well to the left, along a miniature, melting ice cap atop Dead Seal Point.

The spot's name stems, first, from the now vanished elephant seal that died on its seaward side a few years ago. But what is more significant, the rock was once believed to be a peninsular point peeking from under the glacier's foot. Since the 1960s, Anvers Island's glacial mantle has pulled its skirts in by about 30 feet annually. The point turned out to be an island, one of many emerging along the shore. Thirty years ago, the then new Palmer Station was about 50 yards from the same retreating glacial front. Now it is a quarter-mile walk. An eerily beautiful ice cave nearby, today about 40 yards long and formed by a drainage channel along the glacier's base, was twice as long a decade ago.

Lessons for Us All

If you think a few degrees of global warming would not mean much in your neighborhood, the word from Palmer Station is: Think again. While hardly warm here, what with icebergs like ivory cathedrals turning majestically in adjacent Arthur Harbor, it may be the most warmed-up place on the planet. It provides lessons for us all if, as many scientists believe, Earth is unstoppably entering a heat wave that could last centuries.

The Antarctic Peninsula is an S-shaped projection of mountains, geologically related to the Andes, that reaches 800 miles north from the main continent toward South America. The computerized climate models used to forecast global warming reveal no reason for this place to be warming more rapidly than the rest of the planet. But since the mid-1940s, the average year-round temperature on the peninsula has gone up 3 to 4 degrees Fahrenheit, and in the early winter (June in the Southern Hemisphere) it is up a startling 7 to 9 degrees. While it still snows year-round, with summer temperatures averaging a few degrees above freezing and the middle of winter running in the teens, the rate of warming is 10 times the global average.

The bulk of the continent has only warmed a degree or so in the same time. Even this is enough to make some climate scientists worry that a significant part of its ice cap could someday melt, raising sea levels precariously. But there is no sign of that yet, and the South Pole itself, atop a 2-mile-thick layer of ice where temperatures stay well below zero, may actually have cooled a bit. Such inconsistency is among reasons skeptics assert that global warming is too uncertain to merit costly programs to contain it.

Global Warming Is No Hypothesis

But here warming is no mere hypothesis. And one senses how high the stakes are if the skeptics are wrong. The local warm-up is already in the same ballpark as that which the Intergovernmental Panel on Climate Change—set up in 1988 by the United Nations and the World Meteorological Organization to advise politicians—expects for the rest of the world during the next century.

The changes aren't subtle. One hundred miles to the east, on the other side of the Antarctic Peninsula, the immense and supposedly permanent Larsen Ice Shelf began to disintegrate in 1995. Nearly 1,000 square miles of shelf have collapsed just in the past two years, with thousands of square miles more appearing ready to go. "Climate change showed up on the radar screen 30 years ago or so, but most people back then never thought we'd really have to worry about it," says Bill Fraser, a tall, rangy ecologist and penguin specialist from Montana State University. He is the station's chief scientist and has been coming down here for two decades. "Now, right here, we're basically confirming what the models back then said would happen if climate changed. The species most vulnerable, those at the edges of their natural ranges, would be affected first. And that is what is happening."

Lane. © by Cagle Cartoons, Inc. Reproduced by permission.

In recent years, hints of wildlife migrations and local extinctions have been picked up around the world—butterflies moving to new ranges, for instance, or plants moving to higher altitudes on mountains. But the picture here is simpler and starker. Not only is warming greater but, except for the occasional scientist or carefully monitored tourist, direct human impact is scant. So one cannot blame wildlife changes on factors like toxic pollution, agriculture, or urbanization.

And wildlife shifts are unmistakable. Around Palmer and elsewhere on the western side of the peninsula there is not only less ice but a new set of residents. Southern elephant seals—the males are massive, sluglike beasts that can reach 8,800 pounds—usually raise their young farther north in more temperate climes like the Falkland Islands. But one day [in the summer of 1999], 254 elephant seals, including many pups, were seen on just two islands near Palmer, with uncounted others presumably living up and down the coast. More hospitable weather is the only explanation scientists have for this sudden migration southward.

Fur seals, too, were not reported here before midcentury. But [in 1995], a research vessel counted 2,000 of them on just one island farther south. Similarly, gentoo penguins and chinstrap penguins, species common closer to South America but virtually absent in fossil deposits around Palmer, are establishing new colonies on the peninsula. And while nobody expects forests to appear on these icy plains, low grass, tiny shrubs, and mosses are thickening rapidly in many areas of the peninsula.

Investigating the Problem

To see what such rapid heating does to a landscape and its wildlife, a *U.S. News & World Report* team visited Palmer in January [2000], the height of austral summer. The peninsula has no airstrip, so it takes four days from Punta Arenas, Chile, across the Drake Passage aboard the *Laurence M. Gould*, an oceanographic research and resupply vessel under charter to the National Science Foundation. NSF manages the $200 million-per-year U.S. Antarctic program, and Palmer is one of the agency's premier sites for studying long-term ecological change.

At a glance the region looks much as it did to American seal hunter Nathaniel Palmer and other explorers who saw this part of the world in the 1820s. Palmer Station's small cluster of blue, corrugated steel buildings perch upon a rocky shore. Behind them the glacier extends as far as the eye can see. Inside the friendly base are laboratories, warm bunks, a good kitchen, and the "Penguin Pub" bar. Over the pool table is an old whale's rib, and above the fridge is an orange life preserver from the Argentine ship *Bahia Paraiso*, which sank after hitting nearby rocks in 1989. Its hull is still visible from the station at low tide, and it still smells of the oil that wiped out a cormorant colony in the weeks after the wreck. Outside, gale-force winds can pour down the glacier without warning, sucking the warmth from anybody caught outside and not bundled up.

Palmer, with a maximum population of around 40 and an annual cost of $12 million, is one of three U.S. Antarctic stations and the only one on the peninsula. The main U.S. headquarters is McMurdo Station, nearly 2,500 miles away on the Ross Sea, where the population can exceed 1,000 people, and the other station is at the South Pole. Like all of Antarctica, the peninsula is a utopia of international cooperation. No one needs a passport to be here. The 1959 Antarctic Treaty suspended all territorial claims and reserved the great white continent for scientific research.

Fraser, 49, came here as a grad student and soon after did a 14-month sojourn. He makes no secret of the fact that he loves Adelie penguins. Changes here are not limited to new species moving in. Indeed, the Adelies are dying off, and fast.

Imagine a flock of turkeys trying to bleat like sheep, amplify it a few times, and that is the sound of a colony of Adelies. They are packed into nests of small pebbles stained pink with guano, and one often smells their raucous colonies before hearing them. Analysis of debris under nesting sites indicates that Adelies have dominated bird life around here for at least 600 years. And, to a first-time visitor during nesting season, Adelies seem to be waddling comically everywhere on the small offshore islands or slicing swiftly through the waves and dodging fierce leopard seals that prey upon them.

Penguin Problems

But 25 years ago more than 15,000 pairs of the penguins nested yearly within about 2 miles of the base. This year, there are about 7,700 of the handsome, formal-clad couples raising young. The population is down 10 percent in just the past two years. One soon learns to recognize the silent expanses of pebbles that mark extinct colonies.

On Torgersen Island, about half a mile west of Palmer, Fraser quietly watches and counts the birds as they come and go or tend their nests and their chicks. The chicks are about two-thirds the size of an adult and covered in gray down. But in addition to taking a census of the Adelies, Fraser wants to know what the birds are eating. "You know how the old-timers did this?" he asks. He takes aim down an imaginary rifle barrel. "Plink! I just don't think I could ever do that. No way."

Instead, he and co-researcher Donna Patterson select five of the 18-inch-high Adelies as they hop across the rocks, tummies plump from foraging at sea. After a short chase, they drop a net over each bird, pick it up by the base of a flipper, and carefully measure its skull and beak size. While Fraser grips the bird's torso between his knees, Patterson gets behind him to hold its calloused, sharp-nailed feet. Field assistant and graduate student Erik Chapman dips a clear, flexible tube in olive oil. He passes the tube to Fraser, who with a look of apology on his face, slides it down the penguin's throat. Turning a hand crank, Chapman pumps warm salt water into the bird's stomach. In a moment, the bird regurgitates the water, along with its recent meal.

Bird by bird, the researchers fill small plastic bags with disgorged krill, the shrimplike plankton that are the near-exclusive fare of penguins here. Except for a slight pink color from exposure to digestive enzymes and acids, the limp crustaceans look fresh. A pair of brown skuas—powerful predatory relatives of gulls that fly like eagles and often consume stray penguin chicks—alight nearby. They know they'll get some leftovers tossed to the ground by the scientists. As far as can be told, the procedure does the penguins no harm. They endure it with impressive equanimity. Upon release, each scrambles away, flippers flapping, then resumes a deliberate walk back to the colony where mate and offspring wait.

Krill Clues

An hour or so later, Bill, Donna, and Erik are back at a lab bench on Palmer's ground floor, picking through the erstwhile penguin meals with tweezers, measuring each of the krill against a ruler. To the untrained eye they don't look ominous—fat and near the 2.5-inch maximum length that these krill reach. But Fraser sees something else. "This looks bad," he says, laying a few krill upon the lab bench's black surface. Such big krill are at least three years old. Young krill depend in their first winter on shelter under the solid ice that forms on the sea surface. The absence of young krill in these Adelies' diet reinforces Fraser's fear that this food source could collapse if winters around here remain as warm and ice free as they have become. Recently, winter ice is getting rarer. At midcentury 4 out of every 5 winters here produced extensive sea ice. Now, just 2 in 5 bring the heavy winter ice necessary to shelter the young krill.

As early as the mid-'80s, researchers at Palmer could see the local Adelie population dropping. At the same time, chinstrap penguins, almost unknown here before the late 1950s, were (and are) prospering, sometimes walking right into Adelie rookeries and setting up housekeeping flipper to flipper with their cousin species. And while krill may be down, both penguins eat them, so a food shortage seemed an unlikely way to explain their differing fates. Except for a dark line under their beaks, chinstraps look a lot like Adelies. And for a long time scientists knew of no significant behavioral differences between the species that would explain why one might do better than the other. A big clue came in the coldest, darkest months of 1988. That year the U.S.-chartered research vessel *Polar Duke* explored the Weddell Sea on the east side of the Antarctic Peninsula. The expedition, with Fraser on board, found the winter ice pack swarming with Adelie penguins. By contrast, the open sea glittered with chinstraps. Until then nobody knew that Adelies depend on sea ice to get through the winter, feeding on krill around its edges. In recent years, as sea ice has become scarcer around Palmer, it became apparent why the region's Adelies were struggling while the chinstraps flourished.

But that's not the Adelies' only problem. By nature, Adelies are hard-wired for a narrow and inflexible range of behavior, as an anecdote from several winters ago illustrates. The icebreaker encountered perhaps 2,000 Adelies marching along single file. As the ship pulled even with the marchers, the lead bird reached a gap in the ice perhaps a foot across. It hesitated, hopped over, tripped on a small bump, fell flat on

99

its face, popped up, and kept going. "Damned if every single penguin didn't jump at exactly the same place and do a face plant exactly like the first one," Fraser recalls. "Bam, bam, bam." Not one Adelie thought to cross just 5 inches to the left or right. "That says something about the intelligence of Adelies," Fraser said.

This is more than a humorous story to Fraser. It demonstrates that, even more than many other penguins, this species has evolved very inflexible habits. "That is a boon in a fragile and tough environment where, once one finds a good niche, it pays off to stick with it," Fraser explains. "But it is a behavioral flaw in times of climate change."

Reproduction

Around Palmer, he sees evidence on every visit to the rookeries of the Adelies' inability to adjust to surprises. The birds live a dozen years or longer and mate for life. Once a pair establishes a nesting site—most commonly on the same island where they were born and often in the same colony—the couple usually returns to the exact same nesting place year after year.

But warmer air holds more moisture, and in this still-cold place, that means more snow. Prevailing winds here pile snow deepest on the southwest-facing sides of the small islands where the penguins nest. The birds there seem incapable of recognizing, in the deepening snow, that it is time to set up housekeeping somewhere else. When spring arrives in September and October, the Adelies often—and stubbornly—pile pebbles atop snow 2 feet thick or more to build their nests. Later, frigid meltwater kills eggs and newborn chicks by the score. By contrast, chinstraps seem a bit more flexible in where they nest, choosing sites based more on their immediate suitability.

During a penguin-counting survey on Cormorant Island, Patterson points to a tiny remnant Adelie outpost. It has two nests, surrounded by a penumbra of smoothed pebbles where hundreds of penguins raised their young 10 years ago. And standing about insolently are half a dozen brown skuas, waiting for a chance to grab a lightly defended baby penguin. Maps of Adelie colonies consistently show that most of the failed colonies are located where snows have become deepest. The chicks born in these places are hatched later and are smaller. Chicks from colonies on northern-facing shores weigh an average of nearly 7 pounds; those on snowier south shores are a pound lighter. "Lightweight chicks won't survive their first winter," Fraser says.

Every failed penguin colony could be just one more local chapter in the pitiless pageant of nature. Certainly, there are no endangered species here. Adelies are flourishing at the southern end of their range in the Ross Sea. And that fits the climate-change model, too. The Ross Sea historically has been so bitterly cold that a little warming there makes it more, not less, hospitable to the Adelies. "Their whole range," Fraser observes, "seems to be shifting south."

But in most of the world, the natural ranges of species cannot move as easily as they can in this vast, unspoiled continent. If warmer weather drives a species to the edge of a city, or to the top of a mountain, that may be the end of it. And that's why the lessons from the Adelies here should demand attention elsewhere.

Palmer is one of several sites in the Long-Term Ecological Research program, sponsored by NSF to keep track of how wildlife in specific areas is doing. While Fraser has been there longest, other Palmer-based scientists track the richness of the bottom of the food chain, including marine algae and other plankton in the sea, the krill that feed on plankton, and microbes living in the water, ice, and thin soil.

Ozone

Temperature and snowfall are not the only changing environmental factors here, either. The famed ozone hole, a loss of ultraviolet-absorbing ozone molecules in the stratosphere over Antarctica, affects the Palmer area in October and November each year. Ultraviolet radiation levels soar. University of Texas graduate student Jarah Meador found so many bacteria living in the glacier fragments floating in the harbor that she e-mailed Wade Jeffrey of the University of West Florida, principal investigator on a program to monitor the effects of ultraviolet radiation on Antarctic microbes. He had a plan.

One sunny day, after some training in rappelling down ice cliffs with the base search-and-rescue team, Meador hiked up the glacier behind the base and lowered herself on a rope down a narrow crevasse that extended 100 feet into the ice. "It's great down there," she exulted on the way back out. In the deep blue light filtering through the ice, she dug into the vertical wall of ice at intervals, carefully preventing contamination while she gathered samples. If the microbes at great depth turn out to be different from those near the surface, it could mean that evolution is already retuning the microbes to tolerate increased levels of ultraviolet radiation.

No one yet knows how or whether the ozone hole is a major threat to the region's biology. But there is little doubt about warming and penguins. After a few decades watching the same population of birds—he is now studying great grandchicks of some of his first ones—Fraser says he is beginning to feel, in his bones, what he calls ecological time: the decades to centuries over which populations ebb, flow, and sometimes vanish. At one of the station's evening science seminars, physicist Dan Lubin of Scripps Institution of Oceanography, at Palmer to study how ice and open sea reflect sunlight, notes that climate change does not appear or disappear quickly. The atmosphere's carbon dioxide and other solar-energy-trapping gases won't return to preindustrial levels for 200 years or more, even if humans could somehow stop their emissions right now. "Two hundred years!" Fraser says. "Even in ecological time, that is enough to really screw things up."

"*It is by no means clear whether these signs indicate real, worrying proof of manmade . . . climate change, or just regular, naturally occurring variations in the Earth's climate system.*"

Natural Fluctuations Are Causing the Polar Ice Caps to Melt

Jens Bischof

In the following viewpoint scientist Jens Bischof suggests that much of the research into global warming is guided by a presupposition that greenhouse gases caused by human activities such as the burning of fossil fuels cause a rise in Earth's temperature. While sea ice in the Arctic Ocean has indeed been thinning since the 1970s, he argues, no one can say with any certainty what is causing it. Evidence points to the conclusion, he claims, that the melting is a manifestation of a natural fluctuation. Moreover, Bischof contends, the Earth actually could be cooling. Bischof is a research professor at Old Dominion University and the author of *Ice Drift, Ocean Circulation and Climate Change*.

As you read, consider the following questions:
1. According to Bischof, what is the only way to understand long-term natural climate changes?
2. As the author explains it, what is the "albedo"?
3. Why does Bischof believe it is important for scientists to understand past changes in ice drift?

Jens Bischof, "Ice in the Greenhouse: Earth May Be Cooling, Not Warming," *Quest*, vol. 5, January 2002. Copyright © 2002 by Jens Bischof. Reproduced by permission.

Climate change has become a topic of great public interest. Hardly a week goes by without newspaper articles proclaiming global warming, the greenhouse effect, melting polar ice caps and retreating glaciers. No self-respecting weather forecaster can resist the temptation to see a connection between slightly abnormal weather patterns and El Niño, the eternal culprit. And while it is clear that the burning of fossil fuels such as petroleum, coal and wood, and the ensuing rise of carbon dioxide levels in the atmosphere must trigger a reaction of the global climate system, it is completely unknown exactly what kind of reaction will occur.

Indeed, there are signs from some natural systems that global warming is under way. Observations of the pack-ice thickness of the Arctic Ocean from submarines with upward-looking sonar, for example, show a thinning trend since the 1970s. The margin of permafrost is moving north, and the vegetation in the high northern parts of the world is changing toward more temperate forms. But it is by no means clear whether these signs indicate real, worrying proof of manmade, permanent and potentially disastrous climate change, or just regular, naturally occurring variations in the Earth's climate system.

If proven a reality, the most troubling aspect of global warming is that it would cause melting of the polar ice caps, which in turn would cause the global sea level to rise and flood some of the most densely populated regions on Earth. Other effects could be changes in rainfall patterns, which could lead to widespread droughts and threaten agricultural production. One need not be a prophet to imagine the ultimate consequences: forced emigration of unprecedented scale into higher elevations, straining the economies and societies of the involuntary host nations, causing political turmoil and, knowing how humans traditionally react to such changes, most likely war.

But are these assumptions correct? In science, as in other sectors of public life, outcomes of investigations are very often guided, if not determined, by an a priori idea, a tenet. One could also call it a belief. In the case of global warming, this belief is that, if enormous amounts of greenhouse gases are released into the atmosphere, a temperature rise must occur.

This prior assumption has guided scientific thinking and triggered a true deluge of investigations, all desperately trying to prove just that. What has been totally forgotten is the fact that natural climate changes occur as well as manmade ones, and on time scales on the order of decades, in some cases.

Overdue Cold Snap

I believe the only way to detect these changes is from the geologic record of marine sediments. In the high northern latitudes, those sediments contain ice-rafted debris, or IRD. The IRD is deposited on or within ice sheets, portions of which eventually calve as icebergs and then travel on vast ocean currents. The composition and movement of this drifting ice can provide insights into the future direction of climate change. Contrary to the prevailing beliefs inside and out of the scientific community, my studies indicate that warming may not be the direction in which global climate is headed after all.

The last 10,000 years of geological history are referred to as the Holocene Era. During that time, global climate has been relatively stable, with swings from warmer temperatures to cooler and back again. On average, however, there has not been the kind of extreme climate oscillation that has in the distant past led to periods of glaciation. Nevertheless, Earth is overdue for a cold snap. Close examination of the way ice is presently traveling in ocean water, from frigid to warmer regions of the globe, suggests that the mechanisms for widespread planetary cooling may once again be engaging.

Ice rafting is a simple idea: particles such as stones, pebbles and fine grains become embedded in ice. As that ice drifts, it melts, depositing those particles in oceanic sediments, leaving a "drift track" indicative of its source. Geologists are then able to reconstruct past ice-drift directions by finding a method by which particles can be connected to a specific point of origin.

The process of ice rafting is intimately connected to temperature changes on global and regional scales. The physical movement of excessive amounts of ice from polar regions to lower latitudes by shifting ocean currents can lead to substantially lower temperatures. If, for example, the air pressure distribution over the Arctic Ocean was such that winds blew from the Bering Strait across the North Pole toward Fram Strait, then massive amounts of pack ice would be moved into the Norwegian Greenland Sea. In the winter, this process would continuously produce additional sea ice in the open leads created by offshore winds in the Bering Strait region, setting in motion a veritable "ice machine." The regional extent of ice and snow cover in the Greenland Sea would increase, cooling the region, and boosting the albedo, or amount of solar radiation reflected back into space, further amplifying cooling.

"Antarctica Is Getting Colder?"

The data show that one relatively small area called the Antarctic Peninsula is melting and calving huge icebergs. That's what gets reported year after year. But the continent as a whole is getting colder, and the ice is getting thicker.

Michael Crichton, *State of Fear*, 2004.

Depending on the strength and duration, this process could lead to an episode of relatively cold climate over the North Atlantic region, perhaps lasting from a few years up to decades. But if it were sufficiently strong and durable, it could set the stage for global climate to return to full glaciation.

Ice as a Predictor

If sea ice were to thicken and expand by other means, such as cooling forced by celestial mechanisms, including variation in solar radiation or orbital changes, declining temperatures would occur seasonally, during winter and summer but also on much longer time scales, such as thousands and tens of thousands of years. Polar fronts would be pushed toward the Equator. Such cooling is self-perpetuating, increasing the extent of snow- and ice-covered regions, thus augmenting the albedo. The albedo increase, in turn, further amplifies the cooling trend, creating a positive feedback loop that leads to additional cooling, which leads to more ice and snow, higher albedo and more cooling.

Global cooling brought on by ice drift, however, does not require an external motor, such as the periodic variation in the

Earth's orbit that brings it closer to or farther away from the Sun, or a slight change in the tilt of the Earth's axis, also periodic. Rather, a mere change of the ice-drift direction in the Arctic could set cooling on its way, possibly even on a global scale. The geologic record is certainly clear: The climate pendulum has repeatedly swung between a relatively warmer world as we experience today, and glacial climates during which much of Earth was submerged under thick sheets of ice.

In my book *Ice Drift, Ocean Circulation and Climate Change*, I look not just at older data that otherwise would never have seen the light of day but also new data that I believe is persuasive that ice drifting can be as predictive as it is archival. That is, to understand the future, at least in terms of climate, one must understand the past. Any computer model designed to predict future climate change such as greenhouse gas-induced global warming must also reproduce the reconstructed past changes of ice drift in order to be considered reliable. Ice rafting is not just a passive recorder of past surface-ocean circulation, but also actively influences and changes present ocean circulation as well.

At present we do not yet know if the circulation changes occur over one or more decades relevant to humans. This is simply because the low, and in some cases, very low sedimentation rates of the polar oceans do not permit time resolution at these short scales. But recent progress in the analysis of Arctic Ocean sediments has shown that it is possible to find areas with high resolution. This, and the prospect of new equipment in the form of a polar icebreaker able to be on station 200 days per year, hold the promise that the mystery of the driving forces of climate change may be eventually solved.

In the meantime, we should prepare ourselves for the possibility that our cherished ideas about global warming may be, if not dead wrong, only partially correct. Intriguing recent evidence gathered from ice-rafted debris looks remarkably similar to a much older pattern that preceded an ice age. We may have to entertain the possibility that Earth's natural climate development may be on a return to another such period, or at least to colder conditions than we now experience. If so, and ironically, the very greenhouse warming we fear may either mitigate the cooling or cancel it altogether.

"History and science both tell us that a warmer planet has beneficial effects on food production."

Global Warming Benefits Life on Earth

Dennis Avery

In the following viewpoint Dennis Avery argues that a period of modest global warming, such as the Earth has experienced periodically over its history, would benefit humans by making it easier to grow food. In the past, he claims, periods of colder weather have led to poor harvests, famine, and death. But mild temperature increases, he contends, provide more water and more carbon dioxide, which help crops grow. Avery is a former analyst for the U.S. Department of State, and the director of the Center for Global Food Issues at the Hudson Institute, a public policy think tank.

As you read, consider the following questions:

1. According to Avery, why is the Earth's climate more stable during warmer periods?
2. When was the Little Ice Age, as explained by the author?
3. How does warmer weather help the growth of food crops, according to the viewpoint?

O nly in the past 20 years have scientists begun to under-stand that the Earth has a moderate, persistent 1,500-year climate cycle that creates warmings and coolings. Sunspot records and the isotopes of carbon, oxygen and beryl-lium trapped in ice cores and cave stalagmites indicate that this process is driven by a small cycle in the sun's radiance.

The Earth's climate is more stable during warming peri-ods. The warming heats the polar regions more than the equatorial regions, reducing temperature differences and thus reducing the power of storms. For instance, Chinese court records indicate far fewer floods and droughts during the Roman Warming of the first century and the Medieval Warming of the 12th century than during the intervening cold Dark Ages and the recent Little Ice Age.

At the latitudes of New York and Paris, temperatures dur-ing the warm periods rise about 2° C above the mean for 500 to 750 years. Then they fall abruptly about 2 degrees below the mean for a similar period. Thus, the Earth's climate is al-ways warming or cooling.

Climate History: Hot and Cold

Scientists first noted that the Roman and Medieval warmings were part of a much longer pattern when Greenland ice cores, first brought up in 1984, provided 250,000 years of climate history. Evidence of the 1,500-year climate cycles has since been found in Antarctic glaciers, in the seabed sediments of four oceans, in ancient tree rings, and in cave stalagmites on all the continents and New Zealand. But the 1,500-year cycles were too long and too moderate for ancient peoples without thermometers and written records to discern.

In Europe, the Roman Warming of the First Century lasted from 200 B.C. to 600 A.D. It allowed grapes and olives to be grown farther north, and good rains allowed the Ro-mans to buy abundant grain from across the Mediterranean in North Africa. The Roman Warming was followed by the cold Dark Ages (600 to 950 A.D.). Weather is far less stable during the cold phases of the climate cycle. Widespread droughts and storms drove hordes of hungry barbarians to assault the granaries of the collapsing Roman Empire.

The Medieval Warming prevailed from about A.D. 950 to

1300, bringing ample sunshine, milder storms and longer growing seasons. Food harvests were so good that Britain's population rose from an estimated 1.4 million people in the late 11th century to 5 million in 1300. Europe's total population increased from 40 million to 60 million—during a period when temperatures rose higher than today's.

Melting Polar Ice Could Aid Shipping

At the current warming rate, models suggest, the north coasts of Russia and Canada could be ice-free for most of the summer by 2050. Some scenarios suggest the entire ice cap could disappear for a month or more. . . .

It would also make possible the kind of trade routes the world's major shipping companies would find hard to ignore. Today, routes between Asia and Europe require lengthy detours through the Panama or Suez canals.

"If you could steam through [the Arctic Ocean] at container-ship speeds, you could save five days from Asia to Europe," said Walter Parker, a marine-transportation expert and chairman of the Circumpolar Infrastructure Task Force, which paid for the Cambridge workshop.

J. Martin McOmber, *Seattle Times*, January 3, 2005.

From 1300 to 1850, the planet shifted into the Little Ice Age. The good weather ended abruptly. During the summer of 1315, incessant sheets of rain fell from May to August throughout Europe, washing away much of the topsoil and beating crops to the ground. In late summer, the weather turned unseasonably cold, and the soft kernels of the few surviving grain plants were attacked by fungus. Across northern Europe, harvests were disastrous, and famine set in.

"The cries that were heard from the poor would move a stone, as they lay in the street with woe and great complain, swollen with hunger," wrote a Flemish observer. Millions died. There were rumors of cannibalism. The farmers' draft animals starved too, hampering food production for the next decade.

In the coldest part of the Little Ice Age, during the 16th and 17th centuries, famine struck repeatedly. The combination of famine and bubonic plague reduced Britain's population from 5 million to 4 million, and life expectancy dropped from 48 years to 38. The population of the Indian subcontinent dropped from 200 million in A.D. 1200 to 140 million in 1600.

Farmers in the densely populated Low Countries and England were driven to try new farming systems: Multi-ox hitches were invented to pull deep plows through the rich heavy lowland soils, which had defied earlier farmers. They tried new root crops from Asia, such as beets and turnips that could be hoed to keep down weeds—instead of leaving half their fields fallow each year. They grew clover crops more frequently to replace the soil nitrogen taken up by their previous crop plants.

Climate and Agriculture

History and science both tell us that a warmer planet has beneficial effects on food production. It results in longer growing seasons, more sunshine, and more rainfall, while summertime high temperatures change very little. In addition, a warmer planet means milder winters and fewer crop-killing frosts in the late spring and early fall.

The present warming trend has not resulted in agricultural water shortages. Rather, rainfall is currently increasing moderately over most of the world. This is not surprising. Global warming evaporates more water from the oceans, and it falls back down to earth in a reinvigorated hydrological cycle. The Illinois Water Survey tells us that U.S. rainfall has recently risen to match the rainfall of the late 1880s, when the end of the Little Ice Age was still bringing more storminess. Continued warming should enhance rainfall, rather than suppress it. And even if some areas do experience greater aridity under warmer conditions, both nature and humans have been through it many times before, and adapted.

Global warming also brings additional CO_2, which acts like fertilizer for plants. As the planet warms, oceans naturally release huge tonnages of additional CO_2 that dwarf the output from our cars and factories. (Cold water can hold much more of a gas than warmer water.) For plants, it's like letting Lance Armstrong carry an oxygen tank on his racing bike.

Since 1950, during a period of global warming, these factors have helped the world's grain production soar from 700 million tons to more than 2 billion tons last year [2004].

The Benefits of Warming

History shows that a warmer world is better for human health on average. It tends to boost agricultural productivity, which reduces hunger and the illnesses that inadequate nutrition help produce. In addition, weather patterns are generally more stable with fewer catastrophic weather events, and warm weather produces far fewer deaths than cold weather. These factors contribute to longer average life spans and increased human populations during climactic warm periods compared to cooler times.

From the perspective of human health, people have far more to fear from the next full Ice Age than the modest warming that most experts believe the planet will experience in the coming century.

> "*The World Health Organization now projects that millions of people will die from climate-related diseases and other impacts in the next few decades.*"

Global Warming Harms Life on Earth

Ross Gelbspan

In the following viewpoint Ross Gelbspan describes how global warming increases the risk of disease in humans, animals, and plants. Warming temperatures, he argues, allow insects to expand their range into areas once too cold for their survival, enabling them to carry diseases to people and animals with no immunity. Trees are susceptible to the spread of bark beetles whose larvae are no longer killed off in winter due to higher temperatures. Gelbspan is a Pulitzer Prize–winning journalist, and the author of *The Heat Is On* and *Boiling Point*, from which this viewpoint is excerpted.

As you read, consider the following questions:

1. According to biologist Drew Harvell, what is the most surprising thing about climate-sensitive outbreaks of disease?
2. How many people die each year from mosquito-borne malaria, as related by the author?
3. As Gelbspan explains, why have shorter and warmer winters led to an increase in Lyme disease in New England?

Ross Gelbspan, *Boiling Point: How Politicians, Big Oil and Coal, Journalists, and Activists Are Fueling the Climate Crisis—and What We Can Do to Avert Disaster.* Cambridge, MA: Basic Books, 2004. Copyright © 2004 by Ross Gelbspan. Reproduced by permission of Basic Books, a member of Perseus Books, LLC.

There is one group of creatures for whom global warming is a boon. Of all of the systems of nature, one of the most responsive to temperature changes is insects. Warming accelerates the breeding rates and the biting rate of insects. It accelerates the maturation of the pathogens they carry. It expands the range of insects, allowing them to live longer at higher altitudes and higher latitudes. As a result, climate change is fueling the spread of a wide array of insect-borne diseases among populations, species, and entire ecosystems all over the planet.

Those diseases are already passing from ecosystems to people—and the World Health Organization now projects that millions of people will die from climate-related diseases and other impacts in the next few decades.

In 2002, a team of researchers reported that rising temperatures are increasing both the geographical range and the virulence of diseases. The implication is a future of more widespread and devastating epidemics for humans, animals, and plants.

As the *Boston Globe* reported [in 2002]: "Researchers have long accepted that global warming will affect a wide range of organisms, but they are only now beginning to predict what those will be. While climate change scientists have studied a handful of human diseases, [this] report was the first to study dozens of diseases in both humans and nonhumans.

"'We are seeing lots of anecdotes and they are beginning to tell a story,' said Andrew P. Dobson, professor at Princeton University's department of ecology and evolutionary biology and one of the authors. 'It's a much more scary threat than bioterrorism.'"

The researchers reported that the climate-driven spread of diseases will "contribute to population or species declines, especially for generalist pathogens infecting multiple host species. The greatest impacts of disease may result from a relatively small number of emergent pathogens. Epidemics caused when these infect new hosts with little resistance or tolerance may lead to population declines, such as those that followed tree pathogen invasions in North America during the last century.

"The most detectable effects of directional climate warming on disease relate to geographic range expansion of pathogens such as Rift Valley fever, dengue, and Eastern oyster disease. Factors other than climate change—such as changes in land use, vegetation, pollution, or increase in drug-resistant strains—may underlie these range expansions. Nonetheless, the numerous mechanisms linking climate warming and disease spread support the hypothesis that climate warming is contributing to ongoing range expansions.

"What is most surprising is the fact that climate-sensitive outbreaks are happening with so many different types of pathogens—viruses, bacteria, fungi, and parasites—as well as in such a wide range of hosts including corals, oysters, terrestrial plants, birds and humans," wrote lead author Drew Harvell, a Cornell University biologist.

Added Dobson: "Climate change is disrupting natural ecosystems in a way that is making life better for infectious diseases. The accumulation of evidence has us extremely worried. We share diseases with some of these species. The risk for humans is going up."

"This isn't just a question of coral bleaching for a few marine ecologists, nor just a question of malaria for a few health officials—the number of similar increases in disease incidence is astonishing," added another member of the research team, Richard Ostfeld. "We don't want to be alarmist, but we are alarmed."

The risk, of course, is not confined to humans. In Canada, an explosion in the population of tree-killing bark beetles is spreading rapidly through the forests. As of late 2002, the deadly bark beetles had spread throughout an area of British Columbia nearly three-fourths the size of Sweden—about 9 million acres. Officials attributed the spread of the insects to unusually warm winters.

The massive wildfires that devastated southern California in the summer of 2003 were also made more intense by a rapid increase in the population of bark beetles that had killed large numbers of trees, turning them into tinder for the fires that blanketed the area around Los Angeles.

But the impact of the warming-driven population boom of insects on humans is likely to be at least—if not more—severe than the impact on the world's forests.

About 160,000 people currently die each year from the impacts of warming, but the World Health Organization calculates that that figure will rise into the millions in the near future—from the spread of various infectious diseases, increased heat stress, and the warming-driven proliferation of allergens.

Global Warming and International Conflict

The problems of environmental degradation will become far more threatening than they even are today. The ecosystem may not be able to adjust to them. Even if global warming occurs at the slower end of the likely range, its consequences —competition for water supplies, for example, and large-scale migrations—could engender tensions that trigger international and regional conflicts, especially if these are further fuelled by continuing population growth. Moreover, such conflict could be aggravated, perhaps catastrophically, by the increasingly effective disruptive techniques with which novel technology is empowering even small groups.

The interaction of atmosphere and oceans is so complex and uncertain that we can't discount the risk of something much more drastic than the "best guess" rate of global warming. The rise by 2100 could even exceed five degrees. Even worse, the temperature change may not be just in direct (or "linear") proportion to the rise in the carbon dioxide concentration. When some threshold level is reached, there could be a sudden and drastic "flip" to a new pattern of wind and ocean circulation.

Sir Martin Rees, *Our Final Hour*, 2003.

"There is growing evidence that changes in the global climate will have profound effects on the health and well-being of citizens in countries around the world," said Kerstin Leitner, assistant director-general of the World Health Organization.

Start with the bugs. Mosquitoes, which historically could survive no higher than 1,000 meters, are now spreading malaria, dengue, and yellow fever at elevations of 3,200 meters—to populations that have never before been infected and carry no immunity to those diseases.

Mosquitoes are spreading West Nile virus—and not only throughout expanding geographical areas (as of June 2003, West Nile had surfaced in twenty-four states within the

U.S.). They have also spread the disease to more than 230 species of birds, animals, humans, and other insects.

Although West Nile virus has gotten far more attention in the American press, a more familiar disease, malaria, quadrupled worldwide between 1995 and 2000. Today, mosquito-borne malaria kills at least 1 million people and causes more than 300 million acute illnesses each year. In Africa alone, malaria is killing about 3,000 children each day. "Malaria kills an African child every 30 seconds, and remains one of the most important threats to the health of pregnant women and their newborns," according to Carol Bellamy, executive director of the United Nations Children's Fund.

According to [a 2000] article in *Scientific American*, "Diseases relayed by mosquitoes—such as malaria, dengue fever, yellow fever and several kinds of encephalitis—are among those eliciting the greatest concern as the world warms. Mosquitoes acquire disease-causing microorganisms when they take a blood meal from an infected animal or person. Then the pathogen reproduces inside the insects, which may deliver disease-causing doses to the next individuals they bite."

"Mosquito-borne disorders are projected to become increasingly prevalent because their insect carriers, or 'vectors,' are very sensitive to meteorological conditions," wrote Dr. Paul R. Epstein in the cover article of *Scientific American*. "Cold can limit mosquitoes to seasons and regions where temperatures stay above certain minimums. Winter freezing kills many eggs, larvae and adults outright. Anopheles mosquitoes, which transmit malaria parasites, cause sustained outbreaks of malaria only where temperatures routinely exceed 60 degrees Fahrenheit. Similarly, *Aedes aegypti* mosquitoes, responsible for yellow fever and dengue fever, convey virus only where temperatures rarely fall below 50 degrees F."

The problem is that there are very few areas of the planet that are cooling—and many, many areas where the temperature is rising.

Epstein, who is assistant director of the Center for Health and the Global Environment at Harvard Medical School, explained that "mosquitoes proliferate faster and bite more as the air becomes warmer. At the same time, greater heat speeds the rate at which pathogens inside them reproduce and mature. At 68°F, the immature *P. falciparum* parasite takes twenty-six days to develop fully, but at 77°F, it takes only thirteen days. The Anopheles mosquitoes that spread this malaria parasite live only several weeks; warmer temperatures raise the odds that the parasites will mature in time for the mosquitoes to transfer the infection. As whole areas heat up, then, mosquitoes could expand into formerly forbidden territories, bringing illness with them. Further, warmer nighttime and winter temperatures may enable them to cause more disease for longer periods in the areas they already inhabit."

Nor is it only warmer temperatures that propel the spread of insect-borne diseases. Weather extremes, another consequence of climate change, also play a pivotal role. "Intensifying floods and droughts resulting from global warming can each help trigger outbreaks by creating breeding grounds for insects whose dessicated eggs remain viable and hatch in still water," he wrote. As floods recede, he explained, they leave puddles that in times of drought become stagnant pools. As people in dry areas collect water in open containers, these can become incubators for new mosquitoes. The insects can flourish even more if climate change or other processes (such as habitat destruction) reduce the populations of predators that normally feed on mosquitoes.

One very troubling occurrence is that malaria had been declining in the United States before the recent rapid rise in global temperatures. As Epstein explained, "Malaria is reappearing north and south of the tropics. The U.S. has long been home to Anopheles mosquitoes, and malaria circulated here decades ago. By the 1980s mosquito-control programs and other public health measures had restricted the disorder to California."

"Since 1990, however, when the hottest decade on record began, outbreaks of locally transmitted malaria have occurred during hot spells in Texas, Florida, Georgia, Michigan, New Jersey, and New York (as well as in Toronto). These episodes undoubtedly started with a traveler or stowaway mosquito carrying malaria parasites. But the parasites clearly found friendly conditions in the U.S.—enough warmth and humidity, and plenty of mosquitoes able to transport them to victims who had not traveled. Malaria has returned to the Korean peninsula, parts of southern Europe and the former Soviet Union and to the coast of South Africa along the Indian Ocean," Epstein reported.

It will also, scientists report, return to Great Britain. Last year, researchers at Britain's Durham University projected that if current temperature trends persist, the United Kingdom will begin to see recurring outbreaks of malaria in the next few decades.

Nor is the phenomenon limited to malaria.

According to Epstein, "Dengue or 'breakbone' fever (a severe flu-like viral illness that sometimes causes fatal internal bleeding) is spreading as well. Today it afflicts an estimated 50 million to 100 million in the tropics and subtropics (mainly in urban areas and their surroundings). It has broadened its range in the Americas over the past ten years and had reached down to Buenos Aires by the end of the 1990s. It has also found its way to northern Australia. Neither a vaccine nor a specific drug treatment is yet available."

Another insect that flourishes in a warmer world is the tick. In coastal New England—as well as in coastal areas in Scandinavia, researchers have documented a substantial increase in tick-borne Lyme disease. The reasons: The shorter and warmer winters in the northern temperate latitudes are no longer providing the deep, prolonged killing frosts that normally kill the ticks during the winter season.

The changes in the climate affect not only infectious diseases. They are also expected to trigger far more allergies among humans. One team of researchers found that a doubling of carbon dioxide levels—which is expected to occur after 2050—produced 61 percent more pollen than normal. This, in turn, strongly suggests more virulent allergies among current sufferers and new allergies for people who were previously unaffected.

And of course there are the direct effects of heat itself.

Two years ago, the World Meteorological Organization projected a doubling of heat-related deaths in the world's cities within twenty years. "Heat waves are expected to become a major killer," World Meteorological Organization secretary general Godwin Obasi said.

That projection turned prophetic in the summer of 2003. The final death toll of that summer's heat wave in Europe approached 35,000 fatalities, according to the Earth Policy Institute.

Part of the reason for the unusually high number of heat-related deaths—which also occurred in Chicago during a heat wave in 1996, when more than 800 people lost their lives—seems to involve more than rising temperatures. It also apparently reflects the fact that greenhouse gases trap in the heat during the nighttime, preventing the normal radiational cooling that allows heat-stressed bodies to recover from the high daytime temperatures.

Periodical Bibliography

The following articles have been selected to supplement the diverse views presented in this chapter.

Tim Barnett et al.   "The Effects of Climate Change on Water
                         Resources in the West: Introduction and
                         Overview," *Climatic Change*, January 2004.

Paul R. Epstein   "Is Global Warming Harmful to Health?"
                         Scientific American, August 2000.

Sian Green   "Climate Change: Better Off in a Warmer
                         World?" *Power Engineering International*,
                         December 2003.

Margaret Loftus   "Temperature Rising," *National Geographic
                         Traveler*, April 2005.

Jim Motavalli   "Too Darn Hot: Global Warming Accelerates
                         the Spread of Disease," *E: The Environmental
                         Magazine*, November/December 2004.

Bill McKibben   "Driving Global Warming," *Christian Century*,
                         May 16, 2001.

Newsweek International "Winners and Losers: Climate Change Is
                         Shifting the Reproductive and Migratory
                         Patterns of Birds and Other Animals,"
                         September 20, 2004.

Fred Pearce   "Africans Go Back to the Land as Plants
                         Reclaim the Desert," *New Scientist*, September
                         21, 2002.

Douglas Rogers   "Going to Extremes," *Conde Nast Traveler*, May
                         2004.

Margot Roosevelt   "Vanishing Alaska," *Time*, October 4, 2004.

Robert F. Service   "As the West Goes Dry," *Science*, February 20,
                         2004.

Jennifer Vogel   "Extreme Weather: Is Global Warming to
                         Blame?" *E: The Environmental Magazine*,
                         May/June 2005.

C. Wohlforth   "Spruce Bark Beetles and Climate Change,"
                         Alaska Magazine, March 2002.

CHAPTER 4

Should Measures Be Taken to Combat Global Warming?

Chapter Preface

In June 1992 the Second Earth Summit, the largest gathering of world leaders ever held, was convened in Rio de Janeiro, Brazil. An agreement called the United Nations Framework Convention on Climate Change (UNFCCC) was created, recognizing "that the climate system is a shared resource whose stability can be affected by industrial and other emissions of carbon dioxide and other greenhouse gases." UNFCCC called on the world to keep carbon dioxide in the atmosphere from reaching a "dangerous" level by reducing the total emissions of greenhouse gases to 1990 levels. The United States, Canada, and many other developed nations signed and ratified the treaty, and agreed to participate in future meetings to work out details and monitor progress. The third of these meetings, called the Conference of Parties III (COP III), was held in Kyoto, Japan, in 1997.

At the Kyoto meeting, delegates reviewed the UNFCCC and concluded that the suggested reductions were inadequate. Higher targets were set, requiring more reductions from the most industrialized nations. This new agreement, called the Kyoto Protocol, would not go into effect until nations responsible for 55 percent of the total 1990 greenhouse gas emissions ratified it. The United States, responsible for 7 percent, and Canada, responsible for 6 percent, signed the treaty, but the 55 percent target was not yet reached.

Not everyone thought the Kyoto Protocol was sound. Some doubted that global warming is caused by human-made emissions, and they saw no need to reduce energy production and consumption, possibly putting national economies at risk, in an effort that might not affect climate change. Some argued that it was unfair that the treaty called only on industrialized nations to reduce their emissions and excluded poor developing countries like China and India, which produce great quantities of greenhouse gases but would find it more difficult to reduce their consumption. Other environmental groups agreed with British prime minister Tony Blair, who commented that "in truth, Kyoto is not radical enough."

In April 2001 the United States announced that it was withdrawing from the Kyoto Protocol. President George W.

Bush explained that complying with the treaty "would have a negative economic impact, with layoffs of workers and price increases for consumers." It appeared that America's withdrawal would doom the treaty, but in July 2001, at COP VII, delegates from 180 countries finalized rules for implementing the Kyoto Protocol. On November 18, 2004, Russia ratified the agreement, giving the treaty the 55 percent required. The legally binding Kyoto Protocol went into effect on February 16, 2005, requiring the signatories to begin reducing their greenhouse gas emissions.

The Kyoto Treaty is just one of many approaches to global warming. The authors in the following chapter debate the value of the Kyoto Protocol and examine other solutions to global warming.

VIEWPOINT

"Every year of delay in reducing emissions is akin to playing another round of 'global climate roulette.'"

Greenhouse Gas Emissions Should Be Reduced

Fred Krupp

In 2003 U.S. senators John McCain, a Republican, and Joseph Lieberman, a Democrat, proposed a bill calling for mandatory reductions in greenhouse gas emissions. The bill was defeated, but many people believed it generated useful discussion about climate change. In the following viewpoint, originally given as testimony in support of the bill, Fred Krupp explains to a Senate committee that a reduction in greenhouse gas (GHG) emissions is not only essential but also economically feasible. He asserts that action to reduce emissions must be taken immediately, before global warming causes unsolvable problems for future generations. Fred Krupp is president of Environmental Defense, a national organization that works with large corporations to find solutions to environmental problems.

As you read, consider the following questions:

1. According to the author, when should reductions in GHG emissions begin?
2. As the author explains, what kinds of economic activities lead to greenhouse gas emissions?
3. What was the net cost to BP's business after lowering its GHG emissions by 10 percent, as reported by Krupp?

Fred Krupp, testimony before the U.S. Senate Committee on Commerce, Science, and Transportation, Washington, DC, January 8, 2003.

I appreciate the opportunity to testify [before the U.S. Senate] on what Environmental Defense [organization] considers one of the most urgent environmental problems of our time—global climate change. I am very pleased, moreover, that the focus of the hearing is the impressive proposal offered by Senators [John] McCain and [Joseph] Lieberman (shared with Environmental Defense in draft form on December 20 [2002]) to tackle that problem.[1] Finally, I am particularly grateful to this Committee for the previous hearings it has conducted to create a sound, well-balanced record of scientific understanding of global climate change.

Thanks to those hearings, I know that my testimony on the McCain-Lieberman legislation will be considered against a backdrop of increased understanding. First, there is strong scientific consensus that human activities contribute substantially to the buildup of heat-trapping greenhouse gases (GHG) in the atmosphere. Second, if GHG emissions continue to rise, the world will face increasingly devastating environmental disruptions affecting not only our most precious natural ecosystems but also, potentially, the world food supply and human health.

This state of affairs challenges our American values and our American ingenuity. . . .

Climate Change and American Values

Our success in this endeavor will require responsible environmental stewardship—one of the bedrock values held by Americans.

The GHG emissions produced by the first automobile that rolled off the assembly line in Detroit are still in the atmosphere. Each new ton of greenhouse gases emitted today will reside in the atmosphere for decades. Over time, the resulting warming will change the climate—and the environment—in countless ways. Impacts could range from the die-off of coral reefs to the loss of vital fisheries to sharply increased cycles of storms and drought. Sea level rise could be so severe that the entire National Mall here in Washington would be flooded regularly. That this could be the legacy

---

1. The bill was defeated.

of our own everyday actions is a notion that few Americans alive today would knowingly tolerate. America's commitment to caring for our natural heritage prompts us to demand that our national leaders take responsible actions to help curb global warming.

Responsible stewardship requires that we take the necessary steps to protect the climate from the harmful effects of GHG emissions. Because greenhouse gases build up incrementally in the atmosphere, stabilizing their *concentrations* will require very significant reductions in *emissions* over the next century. Moreover, most scientists agree that in order to avoid the kind of drastic environmental damage that most would consider unacceptable, substantial reductions in total GHG emissions must begin *now*. Highly respected analyses indicate that world leaders have a narrow time window in which to act. Failure to begin reducing total GHG emissions within the next decade (the period covered by the McCain-Lieberman bill) may foreclose the chance our children and grandchildren have to avert dangerous climate change in the future.

Climate Change and American Ingenuity

Throughout history, American ingenuity has enabled our nation to triumph over adversity. We need to unleash that same can-do spirit today to help curb global warming. The challenge arises from the fact that GHG emissions are the direct result of fundamental economic activities—like producing energy, food and clothing, transporting ourselves and our goods, using our lands and forests and even creating and sharing data. No matter how powerful our commitment to environmental protection is, unless we can ensure our continued economic prosperity, policies seeking to reduce GHG emissions likely will not succeed.

That's where Americans' ability to solve problems comes in. Achieving significant GHG reductions that the economy can afford will require inventiveness and entrepreneurship. The good news is that climate change *is* a man-made problem, and thus can be addressed by human actions. Our nation's record of success in attaining high levels of environmental protection while enjoying continual economic growth suggests that curbing U.S. GHG emissions not only is eminently affordable, but also could bring about a host of benefits to the public. The best GHG policies will be those that set clear emissions reduction targets and explicitly allow businesses and individuals to seek out a broad mix of the strategies. Through experimentation and innovation, they will devise new technologies and invest in GHG emissions reductions that deliver the biggest environmental and social payoff at lowest cost. At the same time, it is critical that those policies be as close to all-encompassing as possible, so that energy producers, industrial manufacturers, farmers and landowners and other key economic actors have a chance to contribute their expertise to the search for the best ways to reduce GHG emissions.

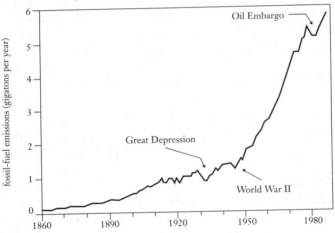

Carbon Injected into the Atmosphere

S. George Philander, *Is the Temperature Rising?* 1998.

This approach reflects more than just blind faith or naïve optimism. Anticipating the eventual need to comply with GHG requirements, many firms and landowners already are experimenting successfully with GHG reduction strategies. Several years ago, DuPont, a charter member of Environmental Defense's Partnership for Climate Action (PCA), announced its intention to cut its GHG emissions by 65% by 2010. In 2001, the company reached, and surpassed, that

128

goal, nine years ahead of schedule. Since 1990, DuPont has succeeded in holding its energy use at 1990 levels. In 2000 alone, the program yielded a $325 million savings; overall the company attributes a $1.65 billion savings to its program.

In Washington State, the Pacific Northwest Direct Seed Association, representing 300 farmers owning 500,000 acres, has joined with Entergy, the power company, to promote direct seeding, a practice that enhances soil carbon sequestration and provides a host of other benefits such as improved soil productivity, reduced erosion and better wildlife habitat. In this partnership, Entergy will lease 30,000 tons of carbon offsets over a ten-year period from participating landowners. In addition to the carbon benefits to the atmosphere, the lands affected by the project will contribute less runoff to nearby waterways, helping to improve the habitat for critical steelhead and salmon runs.

Finally, perhaps the best-known example of can-do success in reducing GHG emissions is that of BP [British Petroleum], the global petrochemical company. In 1998, the company launched a private initiative to reduce its GHG emissions 10% below 1990 levels by 2010. [In 2002], BP announced that it had achieved its target eight years ahead of schedule, and at no net cost to the business, all while achieving steady and robust economic growth.

These are not theoretical models, but real-life actions. In addition to BP, DuPont and Entergy, Environmental Defense has also been working with Alcan, Pechiney, Ontario Power Generation, Suncor and Shell in the Partnership for Climate Action. Each of these firms has established a cap on GHG emissions voluntarily and is undertaking measures to limit emissions to the committed levels. Each company is succeeding in its efforts, while continuing to prosper.

Environmental Stewardship

Environmental Defense believes that the McCain-Lieberman bill embodies America's core commitment to responsible environmental stewardship. First, it would deliver the single most crucial response to the dangers of climate change—actual reductions in GHG emissions below current levels. The current policy debate on climate change features a host of potential approaches, including voluntary initiatives, technology subsidies and tax-like schemes such as cost safety-valves. None of these, however, would accomplish what this bill would do—guarantee actual reductions in GHG emissions. Again, to curb the unwanted effects of climate change means limiting the *concentrations* of greenhouse gases in the atmosphere. GHG concentrations can be limited *only* by reducing actual emissions. McCain-Lieberman would do just that—mandate the reduction of U.S. GHG emissions.

Second, the bill mandates GHG reductions below current levels by the middle of the next decade. Our best analysis suggests that this requirement could keep open the window of opportunity that policy-makers in the future must have if they are to achieve sufficient reductions for ultimate success in curbing climate change over the balance of the century.

Since GHG emissions build up in the atmosphere, every year of delay in reducing emissions is akin to playing another round of "global climate roulette." The ambitious use of emissions trading and flexibility will increase affordability and spur even greater and earlier GHG reductions than are required in the bill as currently drafted. Tightening the reduction levels and timetable now in the bill will only enhance our legacy to future generations. Again, because of the long-lived nature of greenhouse gases in the atmosphere, by achieving even greater reductions sooner, the bill would make it that much easier for future generations to achieve the reductions needed to solve the climate problem on a long-term basis.

"A rash cutback in energy use, as required by [climate treaties], could trigger a prolonged worldwide recession."

Greenhouse Gas Emissions Need Not Be Reduced

Sallie Baliunas

According to Sallie Baliunas in the following viewpoint, evidence that human-caused emissions have contributed to substantial global warming is unconvincing. Natural cycles are responsible for some warming, she argues. Moreover, she contends, acting precipitously to reduce greenhouse gas emissions is likely to cause economic hardship more severe than any hardships caused by modest warming. Baliunas is an astrophysicist, formerly affiliated with the Mount Wilson Observatory. She was profiled in 1991 in *Discover* magazine as one of America's outstanding women scientists.

As you read, consider the following questions:

1. According to the author, how much did the average surface temperature of the Earth increase over the twentieth century?
2. What happened to temperatures between A.D. 800 and A.D. 1200, according to Baliunas?
3. As reported by the author, how much has the United States invested in the scientific study of global warming over the past decade?

The decision to mount America's largest military invasion, the D-Day landing on the Normandy beaches, relied on a weather forecast. Meteorologists studied decades of weather maps from the North Atlantic in order to gain forecasting acumen. Then on June 4, 1944, 5,000 ships carrying 86,000 soldiers crushed against the waters of the English Channel, while 13,000 support aircraft held for an unfavorable June 4 weather forecast. But the June 5 forecasts indicated improved conditions, so Gen. Eisenhower ordered the D-Day invasion for the next day. If that forecast hadn't been accurate, the assault troops might never have reached Normandy's beaches. Thus, modern soldiers have come to know the importance of reliable weather forecasts for technological battlefields.

Today a scientifically accurate understanding of weather and climate is essential for economies built on technology. Human use of coal, oil, natural gas and other fossil fuels has increased the concentration of carbon dioxide in the air. The belief is that this added CO_2 is causing a significant warming of the climate.

The latest report of the U.N.'s [United Nations'] Intergovernmental Panel on Climate Change (IPCC), using several computer simulations, forecasts a human-made global-warming trend between 1.4 and 5.8 degrees C by 2100, with a middle value of about 2.8 degrees C.

To prevent the warming, the Kyoto agreement asks America to drastically cut its CO_2 emissions and energy use by about 40 percent from today's consumption, which surely will yield a worldwide economic disaster. Yet are the forecasts of human-made global warming in the century ahead reliable? Will things turn out as badly as some say? And can cutting back fossil fuel use really reduce global warming?

The answer to the first question is "not very." The second, "not likely." The third, "not much, if anything at all." To know why, we need to look at the scientific record.

Natural Causes or Not?

Yes, CO_2 is a greenhouse gas, which helps keep some of the sun's energy from returning to space. The IPCC forecast of the climate's response to this small amount of extra energy comes from the encoding of present ideas about climate into sophisticated computer simulations. These simulations say that the temperature near the surface and through the first five miles of air, the troposphere, should warm. Has that happened? Compared to the previous five centuries or so, the 20th century did show a warming trend, with a globally averaged surface-temperature rise of 0.5 C.

But look deeper, and the proof of a large human-induced warming dissipates like so much hot air.

First, much of the warming occurred before 1940—before 80 percent of the CO_2 from human activities was added to the air. This means that the early 20th century warming must be mostly natural.

Second, the climate record of the past 1,000 years suggests this temperature rise is hardly unique. New information about historical climate change obtained from trees, glaciers, ice cores, coral and the like indicate a widespread Medieval Warm Period from about 800 to 1200 A.D. Subsequently, climate harshened markedly, creating a Little Ice Age that persisted nearly to the 20th century. So the 20th century's warming seems largely a natural rebound from the cold spell.

But what about the past several decades, when the CO_2 content of the air rose most dramatically?

A critical problem for those claiming human-induced warming is that the computer climate simulations predict both surface temperatures and those of the lower troposphere should rise together. Moreover, the lower troposphere should warm the most.

For more than three decades, surface temperatures actually fell slightly before starting to rise again in the late 1970s. Tropospheric temperatures showed no warming from the inception of measurements by balloon-borne instruments in 1957 until 1976. From 1976 to 1977, an upward shift occurred. But between 1979, after the advent of daily global-satellite measurements of tropospheric temperatures, and the present, neither satellite nor balloon data show a large manmade warming trend.

Proponents of human-made global warming say soot from industries has acted as an aerosol to mask a larger warming trend. But that unravels because whereas CO_2 disperses globally, aerosols tend to stick more closely to where they are released. And the southern hemisphere, which is relatively free of aerosols, actually showed a cooling trend.

Do Not Rush to Control Emissions

Assuming even the worst about the consequences of unabated anthropogenic greenhouse gas emissions and their economic consequences does not necessarily imply that emissions controls today make more sense than emissions controls tomorrow.

There is no compelling need to act now. According to a recent study by Wigley et al. in *Nature*, waiting more than 20 years before taking action to limit anthropogenic greenhouse gas emissions would result in only about a .2 degree Celsius temperature increase spread out over a 100-year period.

Why might we want to wait a couple of decades before acting? First, we might profitably "look before we leap." There are a tremendous number of uncertainties that still need to be settled before we can be reasonably sure that action is warranted. Second, we can't anticipate what sorts of technological advances might occur in the intervening period that might allow far more efficient and less costly control or mitigation strategies than those before us today. Given the low cost of waiting, it would seem only prudent to continue to try to answer the open questions about climate change before making major changes to Western civilization.

Jerry Taylor, "Global Warming: The Anatomy of a Debate," speech to Johns Hopkins University Applied Physics Laboratory, www.cato.org, January 16, 1998.

The point is that the best data collected from satellites and validated by balloons to test the hypothesis of a human-induced global warming from the release of CO_2 into the atmosphere shows no strong trend of increasing temperatures, even as the climate models exaggerated the warmth that ought to have occurred from a build-up in CO_2.

What's Wrong with Models?

Climate models are too simplistic. They must deal with more than 5 million variables, including many that are uncertain or unmeasured. For example, the models lack key information about two major climate effects: water vapor and clouds. Little wonder that these models haven't reproduced the major features of present or past climate, such as the El Niño oscillations, that occur in two- to seven-year periods. They provide no proof that mankind is causing global warming to occur.

But what is causing surface temperatures to rise? A chart of surface temperatures going back more than 240 years shows a strong correlation between them and cycles of the sun's magnetism. Satellite measurements of the past two decades demonstrate the sun is a variable star, with its total energy output changing in step with periodic changes in its magnetism. This correlation suggests that changes in the sun's energy output of a few tenths of a percent over decades may explain many of the temperature changes over past centuries. Measurements made at Mount Wilson Observatory in Los Angeles of hundreds of other sun-like stars indicate the amounts of such changes are entirely possible.

Evidence of substantial greenhouse gas warming is weak. But wouldn't such warming be dangerous? Why not take precautions and cut back our use of fossil fuels?

First, the warming is partly natural, and second, modest warming probably poses less of a threat than cooling would. People benefited from the Medieval Warm Period, with its equable climate conditions, compared to the subsequent deterioration during the Little Ice Age. Fig trees grew in Koln, Germany; vineyards were found in England; and Vikings sailed the seas to colonize Iceland, Greenland and possibly Newfoundland. After the onset of the Little Ice Age, growing seasons shortened, the North Sea became stormier, and life expectancy dropped back by about 10 years due to starvation and harsh weather conditions of a colder climate.

The 20th century's warming has extended growing seasons, too. And increased CO_2 also has helped increase crop yields to feed more people. No deleterious global climate effects can be identified with energy use. Instead, vast numbers of people have been raised from poverty by the economic growth that energy use produces.

By contrast, a rash cutback in energy use, as required by the 1997 Kyoto Protocol could trigger a prolonged worldwide recession. Even economists from the Clinton administration now admit that the price tag for America would run to hundreds of billions of dollars annually. The rising energy prices needed to enforce conservation would especially hurt lower-income workers, who spend a greater proportion of their incomes on energy. And their sacrifice would accomplish little. According to the computer models global-warming alarmists rely upon, temperatures, after implementing the Kyoto Protocol, would decline less than a few tenths Celsius by the year 2100—beneath notice, given the bounds of natural climate change.

America has led the scientific study of global warming with approximately $18 billion in research funding over the past decade. That research shows the threat of catastrophic warming is miniscule against the backdrop of natural change. The best thing now would be to improve the climate simulations and better pinpoint any human effect, while readying cost-effective measures in mitigation and adaptation.

As soldiers can understand, the nation needs a more reliable climate forecast before launching an assault on global warming that could swamp the economy in energy regulations destructive to the world's impoverished.

VIEWPOINT

3

"No matter how strong any Senate mandate, the technology needed to stabilize global atmospheric levels of CO_2 does not exist."

Greenhouse Gas Emissions Cannot Be Reduced with Current Technology

William Kovacs

In the debate over whether greenhouse gas emissions should be reduced, or how quickly, most analysts are missing an important point, according to William Kovacs. In the following viewpoint he argues that no matter how strong the will or the mandate to reduce emissions, the technology needed to accomplish the reduction does not yet exist. The world will still need energy to power factories, homes, and cars, Kovacs explains, and clean alternative energy sources sufficient to supply the power are not now available. Kovacs is vice president for environment, technology, and regulatory affairs at the U.S. Chamber of Commerce.

As you read, consider the following questions:

1. How many terawatts (TW) of carbon-free energy would be needed in order to stabilize atmospheric levels of carbon dioxide at twice today's level, according to an article in *Nature*?
2. According to an article in *Science*, how many wind-energy turbines would be required to produce ten terawatts (TW) of power?
3. Rather than mandating emissions levels, what should Congress turn its attention to, in Kovacs's view?

The climate-change debate rages on with ever more twists and turns, scientists with the Harvard-Smithsonian Center for Astrophysics now find that the 20th century is neither the warmest nor that with the most extreme weather of the last 1,000 years. Harvard scientists also report that the sun may dim in mid-century, producing cooler temperatures.

Despite these findings, environmentalists claim that unless, consistent with the aims of the international Kyoto Protocol, carbon dioxide (CO_2) emissions are reduced to pre-1990 levels, polar ice caps will melt, coastal areas will flood and disasters will abound. Industry counters that computer models predicting such disasters are flawed and that imposing CO_2 emissions limits would limit energy use and be economically disastrous.

Congress has stepped into the fray, and in the next few weeks [in May 2003] the Senate will consider energy-legislation amendments that impose limits on CO_2 emissions from electric utilities and other sources. [The legislation did not pass.]

Unfortunately, there is a major flaw in all this current "fixative" thinking. Simply put, no matter how strong any Senate mandate, the technology needed to stabilize global atmospheric levels of CO_2 does not exist. This crucial fact, noted in science journals, is woefully ignored.

As reported in *Nature*, just to stabilize the atmospheric level of CO_2 at 550 parts-per-million (ppm)—double what it was in pre-industrial times and substantially higher than the present level of about 370 ppm—could require generating as much as 40 terawatts (TW) of carbon-free energy. That is four times the amount of power currently generated by all the fossil fuels in use in the world today. Moreover, as reported in *Science*, policies aiming to constrain CO_2 emissions won't solve the problem because existing technologies have severe deficiencies limiting their use.

The *Science* article notes that producing just 10 TW of carbon-neutral biomass power requires using a land area equivalent to that used by all of human agriculture today, and producing that much power using wind-turbine technology requires building 100 wind-energy turbines, each nearly the size of the Washington Monument, every day for the next 100 years. Analogous problems arise if solar pow-

The Technology Challenge

Nearly everyone agrees [the] Kyoto [Protocol, the international treaty to reduce global warming] represents only a first step in trying to tame the warming of the world's climate that is clearly occurring as a result of human industrial activity. Even the United States probably will be dragged kicking and screaming into reducing its CO_2 emissions, so the issue now becomes one of scale.

In sitting out Kyoto's implementation, however, the U.S. government has forfeited any claim to leadership on this issue, which is likely to be one of the primary drivers of scientific research and technological innovation during the 21st century. . . .

Several studies in Europe indicate tougher standards will drive technological innovation in the area of carbon emissions, reducing the cost of compliance and even creating economic benefits. Great Britain has even promised a reduction far beyond the Kyoto requirements, specifically expecting this kind of technology burst.

In Europe, "the market-based system has gotten off to a great start," [Former Vice President Al] Gore said. "It's based on the simple truth that most of us have long recognized—that the best way to solve a problem involves making certain that market forces work with you and not against you."

Dan Whipple, "Climate: Will Kyoto Leave the U.S. Behind?" *United Press International Perspectives*, February 21, 2005.

---

ered photovoltaic arrays are employed. A further complication is that energy storage capacity needed to balance out intermittently generated power from these technologies does not exist, and no existing effort will produce it. Hydrogen-powered cars are carbon emissions-free, but the demand for platinum to be used in the fuel cells of all the millions of tomorrow's cars far exceeds the world supply of platinum. Fusion could produce more power than any known source except the sun, but fusion research is moving too slowly to meet power demands.

Additionally, developing countries such as China and India, which are large (and growing) emitters of CO_2, will not endanger their economic growth by abandoning the use of coal, a cheap and abundant resource. Simply put, even if the entire industrialized world achieved the CO_2 reductions called for in the international Kyoto Protocol, the overall effect on atmospheric levels of CO_2 would be minimal, and global levels would continue to rise substantially. This is one problem that neither the U.S. Senate nor the Kyoto-ites can legislate away.

Rather than fighting over economically punitive Senate mandates or a largely irrelevant protocol, what is needed is an all out abandonment of near-sighted legislative fixes in favor of a far-reaching [plan] for developing advanced carbon emissions-free technologies that are not now available. If the climate change conundrum is a Gordian knot, technological innovation is the sword that will cleave it through.

Developing, diffusing and deploying needed innovative technologies could take 50 to 100 years. The undertaking could cost trillions of dollars, but investments could be spread over decades. Benefits would accrue to everyone: society, through deployment of technologies that can stabilize atmospheric CO_2 levels; industry, by moving new technologies into the market place; and nations, through technology access, patent and licensing agreements, and creation of stable governmental structures needed to support the endeavor.

Finally, even if serious climate problems do not arise, the effort will lead to new ways to generate large amounts of energy for the continued economic growth of the world economy.

"We must support sustainable, zero-emission alternatives such as nuclear if we are serious about addressing the problem of global warming."

Nuclear Power Can Combat Global Warming

John McCain

In May 2005 Senators John McCain and Joseph Lieberman presented a bill, the Climate Stewardship and Innovation Act of 2005, before the U.S. Senate. It was an updated version of their earlier Climate Stewardship Act. The words *and Innovation* in the title referred to a call for new developments in nuclear power and renewable energy technology. Both versions of the bill were defeated. In the following viewpoint, originally a statement in support of the bill, McCain argues that nuclear power must become an important part of the country's energy future because its generation emits no greenhouse gases, which contribute to global warming. Other alternative energies such as solar and wind power are also non-polluting, but they cannot yet produce a significant amount of energy, according to McCain. McCain serves on the Senate's Commerce, Science, and Transportation Committee, and is a former presidential candidate.

As you read, consider the following questions:

1. According to McCain, what percentage of the greenhouse gases accumulating in the atmosphere can be attributed to the burning of fossil fuels to generate electricity?
2. How long has the U.S. Navy operated nuclear submarines, as reported by the author?

John McCain, introduction of S. 1151 Climate Stewardship and Innovation Act of 2005, Washington, DC, May 26, 2005.

I want to take some time to address the bill's [Climate Stewardship and Innovation Act of 2005] nuclear provisions. Although these provisions are only part of the comprehensive technology package, I am sure they will be the focus of much attention.[1]

I know that some of our friends in the environmental community maintain strong objections to nuclear energy, even though it supplies nearly 20 percent of the electricity generated in the U.S. and much higher proportions in places such as France, Belgium, Sweden and Switzerland—countries that aren't exactly known for their environmental disregard. But the fact is, nuclear is clean, producing zero emissions, while the burning of fossil fuels to generate electricity produces approximately 33 percent of the greenhouse gases accumulating in the atmosphere, and is a major contributor to air pollution affecting our communities.

The idea that nuclear power should play no role in our energy mix is an unsustainable position, particularly given the urgency and magnitude of the threat posed by global warming which most regard as the greatest environmental threat to the planet.

The International Energy Agency estimates that the world's energy consumption is expected to rise over 65 percent within the next 15 years. If the demand for electricity is met using traditional coal-fired power plants, not only will we fail to reduce carbon emissions as necessary, the level of carbon in the atmosphere will skyrocket, intensifying the greenhouse effect and the global warming it produces.

Clean Technologies Must Be Developed

As nuclear plants are decommissioned, the percentage of U.S. electricity produced by this zero emission technology will actually decline. Therefore, at a minimum, we must make efforts to maintain nuclear energy's level of contribution, so that this capacity is not replaced with higher emitting alternatives. I, for one, believe it can and should play an even greater role, not because I have some inordinate love affair with splitting the atom, but for the very simple reason

1. The bill was defeated.

that we must support sustainable, zero-emission alternatives such as nuclear if we are serious about addressing the problem of global warming.

I would like to submit for the record a piece written by Nicholas Kristof of the *New York Times*. Mr. Kristof made the following observation: "It's increasingly clear that the biggest environmental threat we face is actually global warming and that leads to a corollary: nuclear energy is green." He goes on to quote James Lovelock, a British scientist who created the Gaia principle that holds the earth is a self-regulating organism. He quoted Mr. Lovelock as follows: "I am a Green, and I entreat my friends in the movement to drop their wrongheaded objection to nuclear energy. Every year that we continue burning carbon makes it worse for our descendents. Only one immediately available source does not cause global warming, and that is nuclear energy."

I have always been and will remain a committed supporter of solar and renewable energy. Renewables hold great promise, and, indeed, the technology title contains equally strong incentives in their favor. But today solar and renewables account for only about 3 percent of our energy mix. We have a long way to go, and that is one of the objectives of this legislation—to help promote these energy technologies.

Safe and Secure Nuclear Technology

I want to stress nothing in this title [Climate Stewardship and Innovation Act] alters, in any way, the responsibilities and authorities of the Nuclear Regulatory Commission. Safety and security will remain, as they should, paramount in the citing, design, construction and operation of nuclear power plants. And the winnowing effect of the free market, as it should, will still determine which technologies succeed or fail in the market place. But the idea that a zero-emission technology such as nuclear has little or no place in our energy mix is just as antiquated, out-of-step and counter-productive as our continued dependence on fossil fuels. Should it prevail, our climate stewardship and clean air goals will be virtually impossible to meet.

The environmental benefit of nuclear energy is exactly why during his tenure, my friend, Morris Udall, one of the greatest environmental champions the United States has ever

The Impact of Additional Nuclear Energy Generation

Nuclear energy has already made a sizeable contribution to the reduction of GHG [greenhouse gas] emissions in the US. But more must be done and nuclear energy is pointing the way.

A revitalized American nuclear energy industry, producing an additional 10,000 MW [megawatts] from power plant upgrades, plant restarts and productivity gains could assist the electric sector to avoid the emission of 22 million metric tons of carbon per year by 2012, according to the Nuclear Energy Institute—that's 21 per cent of the President's GHG intensity reduction goal.

A doubling of nuclear energy production would make it possible to significantly reduce total GHG emissions nationwide.

While current investment in America's nuclear energy industry languishes, development of commercial plants in other parts of the world is gathering momentum.

In order to create a better environmental and energy secure future, the US must once again renew its leadership in this area.

Patrick Moore, statement to the U.S. Congressional Subcommittee on Energy and Resources, April 28, 2005.

known, sponsored legislation in the House, as I did in the Senate, to develop a standardized nuclear reactor that would maximize safety, security, and efficiency. The Department of Energy has done much of the work called for by that legislation. Now it is time for the logical next steps. The new title of this legislation promotes these steps by authorizing a Federal partnership to develop first of a kind engineering for the latest reactor designs, and then to construct three demonstration plants. Once the demonstration has been made, free-market competition will take it from there. And the bill provides similar partnership mechanisms for the other clean technologies, so we are in no way favoring one technology over another.

No doubt, some people will object to the idea of the Federal Government playing any role in helping demonstrate and commercialize new and beneficial nuclear designs. I have spent 20 years in this body fighting for the responsible use of taxpayer dollars and against porkbarrel spending and corporate welfare. I will continue to do so.

The fact remains that fossil fuels have been subsidized for many decades at levels that can scarcely be calculated. The enormous economic costs of damage caused by air pollution and greenhouse gas emissions to the environment and human health are not factored into the price of power produced by fossil-fueled technologies. Yet it is a cost that we all bear, too often in terms of ill-health and diminished quality of life. That is simply a matter of fact.

It is also inescapable that the ability to "externalize" these costs places clean competitors at a great disadvantage. Based on that fact, and in light of the enormous environmental and economic risk posed by global warming, I believe that providing zero and low emission technologies such as nuclear a boost into the market place where they can compete, and either sink or swim, is responsible public policy, and a matter of simple public necessity, particularly, as we enact a cap on carbon emissions.

The Navy has operated nuclear powered submarines for more than 50 years and has an impressive safety and performance record. The Naval Reactors program has demonstrated that nuclear power can be done safely. One of the underpinnings of its safety record is the approach used in its reactor designs, which is to learn and build upon previous designs. Unfortunately for the commercial nuclear industry, they have not had the opportunity to use such an approach since the industry has not been able to build a reactor in over the past 25 years. This lapse in construction has led us to where we are today with the industry's aging infrastructure. As we have learned from other industries, this in itself represents a great risk to public safety.

Greenhouse Gas Emissions Cannot Be Ignored

I want to close my comments on the nuclear provisions with two thoughts. A recent article in *Technology Review* seems particularly pertinent to those with reservations about nuclear power. It stated: "The best way for doubters to control a new technology is to embrace it, lest it remain in the hands of the enthusiasts."

This is particularly sage advice because, frankly, the facts make it inescapably clear—those who are serious about the problem of global warming are serious about finding a solution. And the role of nuclear energy which has no emissions has to be given due consideration. . . .

Don't simply take my word regarding the magnitude of the global warming problem. Consider the National Academy of Sciences which reported in 2001 that: "Greenhouse gases are accumulating in the Earth's atmosphere as a result of human activities, causing surface air temperatures and subsurface ocean temperatures to rise. Temperatures are, in fact, rising. The changes observed over the last several decades are likely mostly due to human activities."

Also consider the warning on NASA's website which states: "With the possible exception of another world war, a giant asteroid, or an incurable plague, global warming may be the single largest threat to our planet."

Consider the words of the EPA [Environmental Protection Agency] that "Rising global temperatures are expected to raise sea level, and change precipitation and other local climate conditions. Changing regional climate could alter forest, crop yields and water supplies."

And, let's consider the views of President [George W.] Bush's Science Advisor, Dr. John Marburger, who says that, "Global warming exists, and we have to do something about it, and what we have to do about it is reduce carbon dioxide."

Again, the chief science advisor to the President of the United States says that global warming exists, and what we have to do about it is to reduce carbon dioxide.

The Road Ahead

The road ahead on climate change is a difficult and challenging one. However, with the appropriate investments in technology and the innovation process, we can and will prevail. Innovation and technology have helped us face many of our national challenges in the past, and can be equally important in this latest global challenge.

Advocates of the status quo seem to suggest that we do nothing, or next to nothing, about global warming because we don't know how bad the problem might become, and many of the worst effects of climate change are expected to occur in the future. This attitude reflects a selfish, live-for-today attitude unworthy of a great nation, and thankfully, not one practiced by preceding generations of Americans who devoted themselves to securing a bright and prosperous tomorrow for future generations, not just their own.

When looking back at Earth from space, the astronauts of Apollo 11 could see features such as the Great Wall of China and forest fires dotting the globe. They were moved by how small, solitary and fragile the earth looked from space. Our small, solitary and fragile planet is the only one we have and the United States of America is privileged to lead in all areas bearing on the advance of mankind. And lead again, we must, . . . It is our privilege and sacred obligation as Americans.

"While we urgently need to reduce our global warming emissions, nuclear power still remains the least attractive, least economic, and least safe avenue to pursue."

Nuclear Power Should Not Be Used to Combat Global Warming

Coalition of Groups

As the U.S. Congress struggled in the summer of 2005 to find ways to reduce greenhouse gas emissions without harming the economy, many suggested nuclear power as a clean and safe solution to global warming. In the following viewpoint, originally written as an open letter to Congress, the authors argue that nuclear power should not be the focus of U.S. efforts to reduce greenhouse gas emissions. Nuclear power is expensive and dangerous, they claim, and produces toxic waste that cannot be stored safely. Renewable energy sources offer more potential as a solution to global warming, they contend. The viewpoint was signed by 274 environmental, consumer, and safe energy groups, including Greenpeace and the Nuclear Policy Research Institute.

As you read, consider the following questions:

1. According to the authors, how much federal support has the nuclear power industry received over the past fifty years?
2. According to the viewpoint, how many new nuclear reactors would be needed to have a significant effect on global warming?

Public Citizen, "Environmental Statement on Nuclear Energy and Global Warming," www.citizen.org, June 2005.

As national and local environmental, consumer, and safe energy organizations, we have serious and substantive concerns about nuclear energy. While we are committed to tackling the challenge of global warming, we flatly reject the argument that increased investment in nuclear capacity is an acceptable or necessary solution. Instead we can significantly reduce global warming pollution and save consumers money by increasing energy efficiency and shifting to clean, renewable sources of energy.

For at least 30 years, the public, policymakers, and private investors have viewed nuclear power as uneconomical, unsafe, and unnecessary. As a result, no new reactors have been ordered in this country. With respect to these serious concerns, nothing has changed. While we urgently need to reduce our global warming emissions, nuclear power still remains the least attractive, least economic, and least safe avenue to pursue.

Nuclear Power Is Unnecessary

We can meet our future electricity needs and reduce global warming pollution without increasing our reliance on nuclear energy. For example, a 2004 study by Synapse Energy Economics found that the U.S. could reduce carbon dioxide emissions from electricity generation by more than 47 percent by 2025 compared to business as usual and meet projected electricity demand, while saving consumers $36 billion annually. In fact, we can do this while cutting our reliance on nuclear power by nearly half.

The states are moving forward with clean energy solutions. Nineteen states have passed renewable electricity standards requiring an increasing percentage of energy to be generated by renewable energy sources. Replicating this effort nationally would increase our ability to reduce global warming emissions, while benefiting public health, consumers and the environment. Several states are working to increase efficiency standards for appliances, while many are working to reduce global warming pollution from cars. The states are demonstrating that there is an effective arsenal of clean energy solutions that can significantly curb our global warming emissions; it is these ideas that we need to draw upon.

Nuclear Power Is Too Expensive

The economics of nuclear power remain so unattractive that without additional federal subsidies, no new plants will be built. Despite 50 years and more than $150 billion in federal support, the nuclear power industry is still seemingly incapable of building a new plant on its own. In fact, the U.S. DOE's [Department of Energy's] Energy Information Administration stated in its 2005 Annual Energy Outlook that "new [nuclear] plants are not expected to be economical."

Clean and Green—or Obscene?

The splashy full-color advertisements seemed to be everywhere in early 2001: perky kids bobbing to their Walkman stereos, smiling and playing and saying things like "Clean air is so twenty-first century!" You could have been forgiven for thinking the campaign was designed by Greenpeace or Friends of the Earth to attract high schoolers to their cause. In fact, it was bankrolled by the nuclear power industry as part of its stealthy campaign to steal the green high ground. After decades of being pilloried by environmentalists, the industry thought it had finally found a way to attack its opponents' Achilles' heel: global warming. Because nuclear power emits virtually no greenhouse gases, nuclear lobbyists reasoned, it deserves to be applauded as an environmentally friendly energy source.

That clever bit of logic ignores one inconvenient fact: the industry still produces waste that is the most toxic, environmentally unfriendly stuff ever invented by man. Even so, that ad campaign makes clear the industry's strategy for survival. Once free-market arguments are exhausted, its advocates will point to other benefits of nuclear power that they reckon are worth paying for: "security of supply," environmental benefits, and the like. In some countries and in some circumstances, such arguments might have some merit. But is nuclear energy really a special case that deserves subsidies or other sorts of government intervention?

Vijay V. Vaitheeswaran, *Power to the People*, 2003.

Dominion [a Virginia power company] CEO and Chairman Thomas Capps has stated that:

If you announced you were going to build a new nuclear plant, Moody's and Standard & Poor's would assuredly drop your bonds to junk status, hedge funds would be bumping into each other trying to short your stock.

Not surprisingly, private investors have shown such disinterest in supporting new nuclear power plants that the industry is, yet again, at the mercy of federal handouts. In 2003, Senator [Pete] Domenici included extensive federal incentives in his original energy bill, including loan guarantees and power purchase agreements covering up to half the cost of building a new plant, as well as clean air credits and federal lines of credit. Despite this, Standard & Poor's concluded:

> Standard & Poor's Ratings Services has found that an electric utility with a nuclear exposure has weaker credit than one without and can expect to pay more on the margin for credit. Federal support of construction costs will do little to change that reality. Therefore, were a utility to embark on a new or expanded nuclear endeavor, Standard & Poor's would likely revisit its rating on the utility.

Due to the lack of private investment, it is the inevitable that any new nuclear construction will result in significant public cost to taxpayers. Between 1950 and 1998, the federal government spent 56 percent of the energy supply research and development on nuclear energy, while only 11 percent was invested in all renewable technologies. If the federal government is going to spend any money on energy, those dollars should be focused on clean and safe technologies.

Nuclear Energy Is Too Dangerous

Nuclear energy has never been safe, but [after the September 11, 2001, terrorist attacks] nuclear power plants and radioactive waste storage facilities have become terrorist targets as well. Al-Qaeda operatives were surveying nuclear power plants as potential terrorist targets; in the post 9-11 world these risks are only elevated. The National Academy of Sciences has raised serious concerns about the safety of irradiated nuclear fuel storage facilities from terrorist attacks in its report entitled "Safety and Security of Spent Nuclear Fuel Storage." Furthermore, protecting the fuel from terrorists as it is moved to longer term storage facilities, if they are ever built, will be nearly impossible.

The fact that reactors in the U.S. are also deteriorating with age and inadequate oversight by the Nuclear Regulatory Commission provides further reason for concern. Just three years ago, for example, a nuclear reactor in Ohio came within one-fifth of an inch of stainless steel from a rupture that would have vented radioactive steam into the reactor's containment building and could have led to a meltdown.

Nuclear Power Is Too Polluting

Beyond operating concerns remains the unsolved and disturbing issue of waste disposal. Some 95 percent of the radioactivity ever generated in the U.S. is contained in the nation's civilian high-level atomic waste. Despite almost two decades of pushing to make Yucca Mountain in Nevada the nation's high-level waste repository, it has not been shown scientifically to be suitable to safely store the waste. The Yucca Mountain project is further thrown into doubt by the recent revelations of the falsification of scientific data by USGS [U.S. Geological Survey] scientists, as well as the court ruling that found EPA's [Environmental Protection Agency's] public health standards for the site to be illegal. No country in the world has solved its nuclear waste problem. It makes little sense to begin building new reactors when we don't know what to do with the lethal waste from the ones we have.

Using Nuclear Power to Address Global Warming Would Exacerbate the Problems

Major studies, such as those by MIT [Massachusetts Institute of Technology], agree that using nuclear power to have any significant effect on global warming would require building at least 1,000 new reactors worldwide. This would exacerbate all of the problems of the technology: more terrorist targets, more cost (potentially trillions of dollars), less safety, need for a new Yucca Mountain–sized waste site every four or five years, more proliferation of nuclear materials and technologies, dozens of new uranium enrichment plants, and, even then, a severe shortage of uranium even within this century, while displacing the resources needed to ensure a real solution to the global warming issue.

We believe that the financial and safety risks associated with nuclear power are so grave that nuclear power should not be a part of any solution to address global warming. There is no need to jeopardize our health, safety, and economy with increased nuclear power when we have cleaner, cheaper solutions to reduce global warming pollution.

6

"Incorporating renewable energy is one of the most profitable investments many companies can make."

Alternative Energy Sources Should Be Pursued

Lester R. Brown

While the debate over nuclear energy has largely focused on safety, the debate over renewable energy sources has focused on cost. In the following viewpoint Lester R. Brown argues that the potential costs to society from the threat of global warming are so high that nations must find alternatives to carbon-emitting power generation. Wind power could easily supply much of the world's electricity, Brown contends, and the more wind power is developed the less expensive it becomes. Solar energy is also becoming less expensive, he claims, and it is in the interest of governments to subsidize further development. Brown is founder and president of the Earth Policy Institute, which works to achieve an environmentally sustainable economy, and the author of *Plan B: Rescuing a Planet Under Stress and a Civilization in Trouble*, from which this viewpoint was adapted.

As you read, consider the following questions:

1. According to a World Wildlife Fund study, how much money could the United States save each year by shifting from coal to natural gas?
2. Which countries were producing more wind power than the United States by the end of 2002, as related by Brown?
3. How many people in developing countries do not have electricity, according to the author?

Lester R. Brown, "Turning On Renewable Energy," *Mother Jones*, April/May 2004. Copyright © 2004 by Ogden Publications, Inc. All rights reserved. Reproduced by permission.

As world population has doubled and the global economy has expanded sevenfold over the last half-century, our claims on the environment have become excessive. We are asking more of the Earth than it can give on an ongoing basis and creating a "bubble" economy—one in which economic output is artificially inflated by overconsumption of the Earth's natural resources. We are cutting trees faster than they can regenerate, overgrazing rangelands and converting them into deserts, overpumping aquifers and draining rivers dry. On our cropland, erosion exceeds new soil formation slowly depriving the soil of its inherent fertility. We are taking fish from the ocean faster than they can reproduce. We are depleting our nonrenewable fossil fuels and releasing carbon dioxide (CO_2) faster than nature can absorb it, creating a greenhouse effect. As atmospheric CO_2 levels rise, so does the Earth's temperature.

The resulting mega-threat—climate change—is not getting the attention it deserves, particularly from the United States, the nation responsible for one-fourth of all carbon emissions. Washington wants to wait until all the evidence on climate change is in, by which time it will be too late to prevent a wholesale warming of the planet. As the Earth's temperature rises, it affects all life on the planet. Climate change will cause intense heat waves, more destructive storms, lower crop yields, glacier melting and rising seas.

To head off disaster, we must design more efficient transportation systems; raise efficiency standards for buildings, appliances and automobiles; and develop and promote renewable energy technology.

Other Countries Are Cutting Emissions

The good news is that although this is a staggering challenge, it is entirely doable, and many countries are now taking action.

Detailed studies by governments and environmental groups reveal the potential for reducing carbon emissions while saving money in the process. Cutting global carbon emissions in half by 2015 is entirely within range. Ambitious though this seems, it is commensurate with the threat climate change poses.

National and local governments, corporations and environmental groups are coming up with ambitious plans to cut carbon emissions. Prominent among these is a plan by British Prime Minister Tony Blair to reduce carbon emissions 60 percent in the United Kingdom by 2050. Blair and Sweden's Prime Minister, Göran Persson, are jointly urging the European Union to adopt the 60-percent goal, the amount scientists deem necessary to stabilize global atmospheric CO_2 levels.

A plan developed for Canada by the David Suzuki Foundation and the Climate Action Network—Canadian nongovernmental organizations promoting environmental sustainability—would halve carbon emissions by 2030 and would do so only with profitable investments in energy efficiency. This plan was inspired by U.S.-based Interface, the world's largest manufacturer of industrial carpeting. During the 1990s, the company's Canadian affiliate cut its carbon emissions by two-thirds through examining every facet of its business—from electricity consumption to trucking procedures. The company has since saved more than $400,000 a year in energy expenditures. CEO Ray Anderson says, "Interface Canada has reduced greenhouse gas emissions by 64 percent from the peak, and made money in the process, in no small measure because our customers support environmental responsibility."

Another push for renewable energy in Canada comes from the Ontario Clean Air Alliance, an environmental group that has devised a four-pronged strategy to phase out the province's five coal-fired power plants by 2010. Jack Gibbons, director of the Alliance, says of coal burning, "It's a 19th-century fuel that has no place in 21st-century Ontario."

And Germany, which has set the pace for reducing carbon emissions among industrial countries, is now talking about lowering its emissions 40 percent by 2020. This country already is far more energy-efficient than the United States, whose carbon emissions are projected to continue to increase. A lack of leadership, not a lack of technology, is why the United States' goal for cutting carbon emissions contrasts with Germany's.

In April 2003, the World Wildlife Fund released a peer-reviewed analysis that proposed reducing carbon emissions from U.S. electric-power generation 60 percent by 2020. This proposal focuses on more energy-efficient power-generation equipment; more efficient household appliances, industrial motors and other equipment; and a shift from coal to natural gas. If implemented, it could result in national savings averaging $20 billion a year until 2020.

The accelerating rise in the Earth's temperature calls for simultaneously raising efficiency standards and shifting to renewables in order to cut carbon emissions in half. The initial large gains are likely to come with efficiency improvements from mandating efficiency standards for household appliances, automobiles and the construction of new buildings. . . .

Harnessing the Wind

Wind energy offers a powerful alternative to fossil fuels—it is abundant, inexhaustible, widely distributed and clean, which is why it has been the world's fastest-growing energy source over the last decade. Wind energy doesn't produce sulfur dioxide or nitrous oxides that cause acid rain, and it does not disrupt the Earth's climate. It also doesn't generate health-threatening mercury or pollute streams like coal-fired power plants.

Harnessing the wind also is cheap: Advances in wind-turbine design have reduced the cost of wind power to less than 4 cents per kilowatt-hour at prime wind sites—well below the price of nuclear power or coal. On prime sites, wind power can now even compete with gas, currently the cheapest source of electricity generation.

Even more exciting, with each doubling of world wind-generating capacity, costs fall by 15 percent. The recent growth rate of 31 percent a year means costs are dropping by 15 percent about every 30 months.

While natural-gas prices are highly volatile, the cost of wind power is declining. And, there is no OPEC (Organization of the Petroleum Exporting Countries) for wind [so no large group can artificially raise prices].

By the end of 2002, world wind-generating capacity had increased sixfold to 31,100 megawatts—enough to meet the residential needs of Norway, Sweden, Finland, Denmark and

Renewable Energy Can Improve the Environment

Electricity use has a significant impact on the environment. Electricity accounts for less than three percent of US economic activity. Yet, it accounts for more than 26 percent of smog-producing nitrogen oxide emissions, one-third of toxic mercury emissions, some 40 percent of climate-changing carbon dioxide emissions, and 64 percent of acid rain—causing sulfur-dioxide emissions. Renewable energy can reduce these emissions, thereby reducing the cost of hitting any emission caps.

Our analysis found that a 20 percent renewable electricity standard could reduce the projected growth in power plant carbon dioxide emission by more than 50 percent by 2025. Because the 20 percent renewable standard would save money for electricity and gas consumers, these are free (or negative cost) carbon reductions. They represent free insurance against the risk that power plants—the largest source of carbon emissions in the U.S. economy—may have to reduce those emissions someday.

Even most utility executives believe that they will have to implement carbon reductions eventually. Yet in response to the increase in natural gas prices, more than 100 new coal-fired power plants have been proposed. These plants will expose their owners, power purchasers, and customers to the risk of future price increases that could be avoided by investing in renewable energy instead.

Indeed, under an economy-wide cap-and-trade approach, the carbon reductions from increasing renewable energy will save money for every sector of the economy.

Whether you think that risk of climate change is great or small, increasing renewable energy can reduce the risk of responding to it. And renewable energy reduces emissions of sulfur dioxide, nitrogen oxides, particulates, and mercury, reducing the cost of complying with emission reduction requirements for these pollutants as well.

Alan Nogee, testimony before U.S. House Energy and Commerce Committee, February 16, 2005.

Belgium combined. Germany, with more than 12,000 megawatts of wind power at the end of 2002, leads the world in generating capacity. Spain and the United States, at 4,800 and 4,700 megawatts, are second and third respectively. Tiny Denmark is fourth with 2,900 megawatts, and India is fifth with 1,700 megawatts. A second wave of major players is coming onto the field, including the United Kingdom, France, Italy, Brazil and China. Europe has enough easily accessible offshore wind energy to meet all of its electricity needs, and China can easily double its current electricity generation from wind alone.

Globally, ambitious efforts to develop wind power are beginning to take shape. Germany is proposing a 30-percent cut in greenhouse-gas emissions throughout Europe by 2020—developing the continent's wind-energy resources is at the heart of this carbon-reduction effort. And the United States is following Europe's lead. A 3,000-megawatt wind farm in South Dakota, designed to partly power the industrial Midwest surrounding Chicago, is one of the largest energy projects of any kind. Cape Wind is planning a 420-megawatt wind farm off the coast of Cape Cod, Massachusetts, and a newly formed energy company, called Winergy, has plans for some 9,000 megawatts in a network of wind farms stretching along the Atlantic coast.

In the United States, a national wind-resource inventory published in 1991 indicates enough harnessable wind energy exists in just three states—North Dakota, Kansas and Texas—to satisfy national electricity needs. Today, this greatly understates U.S. potential: Recent advances in wind-turbine design and size have dramatically expanded the wind-power industry.

It is time to consider an all-out effort to develop wind resources, given the enormous wind-generating potential and the associated benefits of climate stabilization. Instead of doubling wind-power generation every 30 months or so, perhaps we should aim to double wind-electric generation each year for the next several years. Costs would drop precipitously, giving wind-generated electricity an even greater advantage over fossil fuels.

Cheap electricity from wind is likely to become the principle source for electrolyzing water to produce hydrogen. Hydrogen can be transported through pipelines to power residential and industrial buildings; it also can be stored in power plants and used when the wind ebbs. The hydrogen storage and distribution system—most likely an adaptation of existing natural-gas systems—provides a way of both storing and transporting wind energy.

The incentives for switching to a wind/hydrogen system could come partly from restructuring global energy subsidies—shifting the $210 billion in annual fossil-fuel subsidies to the development of wind energy, hydrogen generators and kits to convert engines from gasoline to hydrogen. The investment capital could come from private capital markets and from companies already in the energy business: Energy giants Shell and BP have begun investing in wind power, and major corporations such as General Electric and ABB, a company that produces technology systems, are now in the wind-power business.

Solar Energy Rises

In recent years, a vast new market for solar power has opened in developing nations that are not yet linked to an electrical grid. About 1.7 billion people in developing nations do not have electricity, but as the cost of solar cells declines, it often is cheaper to provide electricity from solar cells than from a centralized source.

In Andean villages, solar-power systems are replacing candles. For villagers paying installation costs over 30 months, the monthly payment is roughly the same as the cost of a month's supply of candles. Once the solar cells are paid for, the villagers essentially have a free source of power that can supply electricity for decades. . . .

The residential use of solar cells also is expanding in industrial countries. In Japan, where companies have commercialized a solar roofing material, some 70,000 homes now have solar installations. Consumers in Germany receive low-interest loans and a favorable guaranteed price when feeding excess electricity into the grid. In industrial nations most installations reduce the consumer's dependence on grid-supplied electricity, much of it originating from coal.

The governments with the strongest incentives for solar cells have the largest solar-cell manufacturing industries. Japan leads in solar-cell manufacturing and controls 43 percent of the global solar-cell market; residential installations produced roughly 100 megawatts in 2001. Germany produced 75 megawatts that year, and the European Union, led by Germany's vigorous program, is in second place behind Japan with 25 percent of the world's total output. The United States is third—with 32 megawatts of installations and 24 percent of the market. India is fourth with 18 megawatts.

Solar-generated electricity still is much more costly than power from wind or coal-fired plants, but industry experts estimate that with each doubling of cumulative production, the price drops roughly 20 percent. Over the last seven years, solar-cell sales expanded an average of 31 percent annually, doubling every 2.6 years.

Only modest government incentives are needed to accelerate the growth of solar power and make it a major player in the world energy economy.

Building the Hydrogen Economy

The evolution of the fuel cell—a device that uses an electrochemical process to convert hydrogen into electricity—is setting the stage for the evolution of a hydrogen-based economy. The fuel cell is twice as efficient as the internal combustion engine and emits only water vapor. The fuel cell facilitates the shift to a single fuel—hydrogen—that neither pollutes nor disrupts the Earth's climate. Stationary fuel cells can be installed in the basements of buildings to heat, cool and generate electricity for lights and appliances. Mobile fuel cells can power cars and portable electronic devices, such as cell phones and laptop computers. Hydrogen can come from many sources, including water, natural gas or gasoline. . . .

In the end, the central question with hydrogen is whether it is made using renewable energy to electrolyze water, or with climate-disrupting fossil fuels. Natural gas likely will be the main source of hydrogen in the near future, but, given its abundance, wind has the potential to become the principal source in the new energy economy. The hydrogen storage and distribution system provides ways of storing and transporting wind energy efficiently—it is a natural marriage. Thus, countries that are rich in wind and rather sparsely populated, such as Canada, Argentina and Russia, could export hydrogen. Eastern Siberia, for example, could supply vast amounts of hydrogen to China, South Korea and Japan.

In the United States, energy consultant Harry Braun made a proposal at an April 2003 Renewable Hydrogen Roundtable to quickly shift to a wind/hydrogen economy. He noted that if wind turbines were mass-produced like automobiles, the cost of wind-generated electricity would drop to 1 or 2 cents per kilowatt-hour.

Rather than wait for fuel cell engines, Braun suggests using hydrogen in internal combustion engines of the sort developed by German auto manufacturer BMW. He calculates that the production of hydrogen and high-efficiency, hydrogen-fueled engines would bring the cost of hydrogen down to $1.40 per equivalent-gallon of gasoline. If we make this conversion a priority, it can happen in two to three years.

Building a Better Future

In looking at new energy sources, wind seems certain to be the centerpiece in the new energy economy. Its wide distribution offers a practical alternative to oil, and the industry has evolved to the point where it can expand dramatically over the next decade and become the world's leading electricity source. If you think change can't happen that fast, just look at the recent adoption of other popular technologies, such as cell phones. In 1990, 11 million cell phones were in use globally. By 2002, the number had reached 1.2 billion, outnumbering the 1.1 billion fixed-line phones. In 12 years, cell phones went from being a novelty to dominating the market—their sales growth illustrates how market forces can drive the adoption of an appealing technology. The cell-phone market grew by 50 percent a year during the 1990s; wind power has grown 31 percent per year since 1995.

If we decided for climate-stabilization reasons that we wanted to double wind-electric generation each year, wind could become the dominant source of electricity. The United States, for example, now has nearly 5,000 megawatts of wind-generating capacity. Doubling that each year would take it to 640,000 megawatts in seven years and make it the leading source of electricity. And this is not beyond the capacity of the industry: In 2001, wind-electric generating capacity grew by 67 percent. The total investment needed to reach this level of generation, using the rule of thumb of $1 million per megawatt (which is now on the high side), would be $640 billion over a seven-year span, or roughly $90 billion a year. For perspective, Americans currently spend $190 billion a year on gasoline.

While subsidies are being shifted from fossil fuels to renewables and the hydrogen economy infrastructure, it would make eminent sense to reduce income taxes and raise taxes on climate-disrupting energy sources at the same time. This tax shifting, already under way in several nations in Europe, helps consumers of energy—both individuals and corporations—understand the full costs of burning fossil fuels.

Although shifting subsidies and taxes are at the heart of the energy transformation that is needed, other policy tools can either increase efficiency or accelerate the shift to renewables and the hydrogen-based economy. For instance, national and local governments, corporations, universities and individual homeowners can buy green power. In the United States, even if green power is not offered locally, a national Green Power Partnership electricity market operated by the Environmental Protection Agency enables anyone to buy green power. As more users sign up, the incentive for energy companies to produce green power increases.

As wind energy expands, the next step would be to close coal-fired power plants or use them to back up wind. Coal-fired plants are the most climate-disruptive energy source because coal is almost pure carbon. Coal burning also is the principal source of the mercury deposits that contaminate freshwater lakes and streams. The prevalence of mercury-contaminated fish has led 44 state governments in the United States to issue warnings to consumers to limit or avoid eating fish from their locales. In 2001, the Centers for Disease Control and Prevention warned that 375,000 babies born each year in the United States are at risk of impaired mental development because of mercury exposure.

Although some industry groups and governmental bodies complain that reducing carbon emissions is costly and a burden on the economy, study after study concludes it is possible to reduce carbon emissions while making money in the process. The experience of individual companies confirms this. DuPont, one of the world's largest chemical manufacturers, already has cut its greenhouse-gas emissions from its 1990 level by 65 percent. In an annual report, CEO Charles Holliday Jr. proudly reports savings of $1.5 billion in energy-efficiency gains from 1990 to 2002.

It has become clear that incorporating renewable energy is one of the most profitable investments many companies can make, and as the true costs of climate change—withering crops, rising sea levels and wildlife extinction—become apparent, companies that ignore need to phase out fossil fuels will ultimately disappear. The companies that prosper will be the ones that adapt to a modern economy fueled by clean, renewable energy.

*"Replacing conventional energy sources
with renewable energy would be more
costly and less efficient than other emission
abatement strategies."*

Alternative Energy Should Not Be Pursued

Jerry Taylor and Peter VanDoren

Advocates of renewable energy sources such as wind and solar power believe that they could power the world without
producing harmful greenhouse gases. However, in the following viewpoint Jerry Taylor and Peter VanDoren argue
that the high cost of these energy sources overrides their potential benefits. Generating electricity through wind power,
for example, is much more expensive than generating the
same amount of electricity using coal or natural gas, they
claim. Government subsidies help bring the prices for renewables down, they contend, but this is not a good use of
government money because global warming—and therefore
the advantage of using renewables—is unproven. Taylor is
director of natural resource studies at the Cato Institute, a
conservative think tank. VanDoren is the editor of Cato's
Regulation magazine and an expert in political economy.

As you read, consider the following questions:

1. What percentage of total U.S. electricity comes from
   solar, wind, geothermal, and biomass, according to the
   viewpoint?
2. In what ways are consumers already sharing the cost of
   the pollution caused by coal-burning electrical plants, as
   explained by Taylor and VanDoren?

Jerry Taylor and Peter VanDoren, "Evaluating the Case for Renewable Energy: Is
Government Support Warranted?" *Cato Institute Policy Analysis*, January 10, 2002.

Solar, wind, geothermal, and biomass energy are used in about 2 percent of total U.S. electricity generation and are expected to produce only 2.8 percent by 2020. The use of renewable energy and forecasts of its growth are low because the cost of renewable energy-fired electricity is greater than that of its main competitor, combined-cycle natural gas. Few analysts believe that this will change any time soon.

Renewable energy sources are also capital intensive compared with combined-cycle natural gas. In deregulated electricity markets, investors lack any guarantee that capital costs will be recovered from customers. Accordingly, investors favor technologies that have higher marginal but lower capital costs, such as combined-cycle natural gas.

Advocates of renewable energy argue that the demand for renewables would rise if conventionally generated electricity were priced to reflect its pollution costs. But a reasonable interpretation of the evidence suggests that the additional cost of further pollution reduction would exceed the additional health benefits. Even if current regulatory costs are insufficiently reflective of true environmental costs, "getting prices right" will not significantly affect consumer choices of fuel. For example, reducing emissions of nitrogen oxides and sulfur dioxide by 75 percent below 1997 levels would increase electricity prices by only about 1 percent, too little to trigger a shift from coal or natural gas to renewable energy.

Cracking down on greenhouse gas emissions to comply with the Kyoto Protocol would provide economic help for renewable energy technologies, but such initiatives would result in only a 7 percent market share for renewable energy and a 43 percent increase in electricity prices in return for benefits that are still very uncertain.

Renewables Cannot Compete

Ever since the energy crises of the 1970s, the U.S. government has promoted the use of "renewable energies"—primarily wind, solar, biomass (burning wood and plant material for power), and geothermal (tapping the hot steam or rock beneath the earth)—as desirable substitutes for conventional fossil fuels. Renewable energy (which, for the purposes of this paper, does not include nuclear power or hydropower) is widely thought to be not only more environmentally benign than coal or oil but also nearly as attractive economically.

The state and federal campaign to promote the use of renewable energy, however, has not yet significantly affected electricity generation patterns. Since the establishment of the U.S. Department of Energy in 1978, the federal government has spent more than $11 billion to subsidize—via investment tax credits, production credits, accelerated depreciation of capital costs, publicly funded research and development (R&D), and mandatory purchases at avoided cost—wind, solar, biomass, and geothermal power. Yet those fuels account for only a tiny share of the electricity produced.

The Trouble with Wind Power

Society must still have a guaranteed electrical supply available to power factories, homes, offices, schools, hospitals etc. 24 hours each day and every day, even when these alternatives cannot supply power to the grid. And that supply . . . must be kept spinning continuously, ready to kick in to meet demand. In other words, why throw hundreds of millions of dollars into an unpredictable, intermittent and uncontrolled electrical supply from windmills which do not supply electricity when the wind does not blow, and are surplus to those facilities that you must have operational anyway? If we wish to really conserve energy and resources, we can conserve windmills. Don't build them.

John K. Sutherland, *Times and Transcript*, May 23, 2005.

Advocates of renewable energy continue to insist that it is poised to gain significant market share over the next several years. Although renewable energy is still more expensive than conventional energy, production costs have come down significantly over the past 22 years, and the gap between the cost of conventional and renewable energy has narrowed substantially. And if nations reduce greenhouse gas emissions, environmentalists argue, renewables will become the lowest-cost sources of electricity fuel on the market.

This study examines the economics of renewable energy in the electricity market and the case for government intervention to promote its use. We reach three conclusions:

• Renewable energy is not likely to gain significant market share in the foreseeable future without a significant increase in government subsidies or mandates.

• Rationales for subsidies for renewable energy and other preferences are without sound economic foundation.

• The threat of global warming is speculative, and such warming is not necessarily deleterious from an economic perspective. Even if restrictions on greenhouse gas emissions were necessary, replacing conventional energy sources with renewable energy would be more costly and less efficient than other emission abatement strategies.

The Economics of Renewable Energy

Although renewable energy is often thought of as an "infant industry" facing an uphill and unfair struggle against "Big Oil" and the coal industry, the truth is that the largest corporate conglomerates in America have long devoted themselves to making renewable energy markets a reality. Starting in the mid-1970s, Exxon, Shell, Mobil, ARCO, Amoco, General Electric, General Motors, Texas Instruments, and Grumman all initiated aggressive renewable energy R&D projects.

The widespread belief that oil companies have incentives to stymie advances in renewable energy is belied not only by such facts; it's also belied by the economics of the electricity industry. According to the Energy Information Administration [EIA], a semi-independent agency of the U.S. Department of Energy, oil, which is primarily a transportation fuel, does not compete with renewable energy, which is primarily an electricity fuel.

The most aggressive renewable energy development initiatives today continue to be undertaken by large multinational corporations. In the United States, Zond Energy Systems, owned by Enron Corporation (once the world's largest integrated natural gas company with 1997 revenues of $20 billion), is the largest domestic wind turbine manufacturer and the only manufacturer of large-capacity turbines (those typically installed by electric generating companies). Likewise, 65 percent of the global market for photovoltaic cells (the key component of most solar power facilities) in 1999 was dominated by five large multinational corporations: British Petroleum, Kyocera, Sharp, Siemens, and Sanyo (in descending order of market share).

To advocates of renewable energy, heavy corporate investment in renewable energy technologies is evidence of the potential competitiveness of alternative fuels in the near future. But some perspective is necessary. Total private-sector investment in solar, wind, and biomass energy in 1995 was less than 1 percent of total world energy investments. Royal Dutch Shell's highly publicized planned expenditure of from $500 million to $1 billion on renewable energy development, for instance, is at most 10 percent of the corporation's $10 billion capital spending budget. . . .

Solar, wind, geothermal, and biomass energy account for only about 2 percent of total U.S. electricity generation, according to the most recent data.

Cost Data

Accurate estimates of the cost of renewable energies are surprisingly hard to obtain. A 1997 study undertaken jointly by the U.S. Department of Energy and the Electric Power Research Institute argued that no renewable energy source was competitive with combined-cycle natural gas turbine technology, the primary source of new electric power capacity, which produces electricity at about 3 cents per kilowatt-hour (kWh).

Renewable energy costs, however, include numerous government subsidies and preferences that mask the true cost of generating electricity from those sources. The impact of preferences varies by fuel source and facility, but they reduce the true cost of renewable energy production by at least 2 cents per kWh. . . .

Without policy privileges, the renewable energy industry (at least the portion that generates electricity for the power grid) would cease to exist. For instance, Christine Real de Azua, an analyst at the Wind Energy Association, concedes that "the fact remains that wind energy, while close to being competitive with conventional generating technologies . . . was still not competitive enough [as of 1998] to win all-source bids from utilities in the absence of policies that either created a steady assured market for renewable energy, or ensured that its environmental attributes were adequately captured and valued in the marketplace." Stanford University engineers Mark Jacobson and Gilbert Masters concede that wind is competitive only if government intervenes to internalize environmental externalities of conventional electricity production. . . .

Production costs of renewable energy vary tremendously by location. Ideal sites will produce lower-cost power, but the number of ideal sites in the United States (and, indeed, in the world) is limited, a consideration so fundamental to the economics of wind power, for example, that the EIA states bluntly that "because of limits to windy land area, wind is considered a finite resource." Moreover, ideal sites will be developed before higher-cost sites, so the expected trajectory should be rising, not decreasing, costs, all other things being equal.

Finally, production costs and generation capacity of wind and solar power facilities are heavily dependent on weather conditions, which makes those energy sources unsuitable for continuous, or baseload, generation. For example, Traverse City Light & Power installed one of the largest wind generators in the country in 1996. But wind speeds have been 15–20 percent below projected averages, and the plant has produced only 67 percent of the electricity anticipated. The turbine was particularly unproductive during the summer months when peak demand was highest.

"Green Power" Offerings in a Deregulated Market

While renewable energy is more expensive than conventionally generated energy, public opinion polls continue to suggest that consumers are willing to pay higher energy costs if doing so will improve environmental quality. Accordingly, a number of independent power marketers in seven states have packaged "green power" electricity plans (made up almost entirely of wind-fired electricity) and marketed those plans to ratepayers in states that give consumers the right to choose their power suppliers.

Eighty utilities in 28 states also offer special packages of renewable energy to ratepayers at a premium. "Green power" costs from 0.4 cents to 20 cents per kWh more than conventional power in these plans, with a median premium of 2.5 cents per kWh. Because of higher costs, no more than 1.5 percent of the retail customers in any state have signed up for such independently marketed programs, and participation in utility-sponsored programs is generally around 1 percent or less. Clearly, there is a difference between what people tell pollsters about their "willingness to pay" for environmental quality and their actual willingness to pay in the marketplace.

While consumer preferences may change, even advocates of renewable energy concede that, until renewable-fired electricity costs become comparable to those of conventional energy, green marketing programs are unlikely to attract many customers.

Forecasts for Growth

Advocates of renewable energy often use recent trends in the wind industry—a growth rate of nearly 70 percent from 1997 through 2000, for example—as the basis for predictions about future growth potential. But such arguments can be charitably described as boosterism.

The EIA generates predictions using the National Energy Modeling Systems, a sophisticated computer model of the industry that is used to forecast changes in energy markets. NEMS forecasts are far less optimistic about the near or midterm prospects for renewable energy than are the forecasts of advocates of renewable energy. . . .

Fossil Fuel Electricity Costs

Generation of electricity from renewables is limited by costs. Advocates of renewable energy know this so they argue that the demand for renewables would rise if conventionally generated electricity were priced to reflect its pollution costs.

The argument that fossil fuel extraction and combustion foul the environment in ways that are incompatible with property rights and markets has some merit. Air and water resources have been treated as a public commons rather than as private property. Advocates of renewable energy argue that consumers of fossil fuels have not had to indemnify anyone for the environmental consequences of their consump-

171

tion and thus prices for fossil fuels are too low. Consequently, society consumes "too much" fossil fuel.

Although a world of relatively "unpriced" pollution existed prior to 1970 and the enactment of the Clean Air Act amendments, environmental regulation since the 1970s has imposed large costs on firms, particularly new coal-burning utilities, and those costs have been passed on to consumers. So, in a sense, consumers of electricity *have* had to pay a premium for the environmental consequences of the fossil fuels they consume. For example, the costs of compliance with the Clean Air Act through the 1970s and 1980s (the "environmental tax" on fossil fuels) were about $25 billion to $35 billion annually. The relevant question, then, is whether the regulatory cost paid by consumers already covers the environmental "cost" of fossil fuel consumption.

The answer, unfortunately, is not at all clear. The estimates of the economic damage caused by fossil fuel consumption are all over the map. If we accept EPA's estimates as a reasonable point of analytic departure, however, we find that biomass and coal are somewhat undertaxed relative to their external costs, natural gas is substantially overtaxed, and gasoline is taxed correctly.

But analysis cannot stop there. Economic efficiency—the explicit goal of advocates of renewable energy who cite market failure as a rationale for government intervention—requires that the additional benefits obtained from expenditures for pollution abatement exceed the additional costs. Subsidies to renewable energy sources are necessary to correct for the costs of air pollution *if and only if* incremental net benefits would arise from reduced pollution relative to the status quo. And even then an economically justified subsidy would equal only the *difference* between the existing prices of fossil fuels (which include the cost of existing pollution controls as well as some taxes) and a price that included all pollution damages. Most analysts, however, conclude that the incremental costs of air pollution controls established over the past decade have far exceeded the incremental benefits.

Because pollution policies already control emissions and a reasonable interpretation of the evidence suggests that the additional cost of further exposure reduction exceeds the additional health benefits, the economically efficient subsidy for alternative electricity sources is probably zero.

Even if current regulatory costs are insufficiently reflective of true environmental costs, they are not so far off the mark that "getting prices right" would significantly affect consumer decisions about fuels. The U.S. General Accounting Office reported,

> The consideration of externalities in the planning process for electricity has generally had no effect on the selection or acquisition of renewable energy sources [because] electricity from renewable energy usually costs so much more than electricity from fossil fuels that externality considerations do not overcome the difference.

Moreover, as we'll see below, tightening environmental regulations on coal- and gas-fired power plants would have little effect on renewable energy's ability to compete in the electricity marketplace.

Does Global Warming Alter the Conclusion?

Does the threat of global warming alter the conclusion of the last section? This study will not provide a thorough review of the scientific disputes surrounding global climate change, but scientists do not agree on whether anthropogenic greenhouse gases will have a significant deleterious effect on either the economy or the environment.

Even if the scientific alarmists are correct about the effects of anthropogenic greenhouse gas emissions, it is not clear that the benefits of restricting fossil fuel consumption outweigh the costs. And unless the benefits of "doing something" about global warming outweigh the costs, the efficient greenhouse gas "tax" on coal- or gas-fired electricity is zero.

Accordingly, the case for promoting renewable energy to "do something" about global warming is empirically weak. Moreover, as we discussed earlier, embracing a policy of "doing something" about global warming does not necessarily translate into a policy of subsidizing renewable energy; there are far less costly means of reaching that end.

"If Kyoto encourages the hunt for . . . new technologies—as it has—that is worth something."

The Kyoto Protocol Can Help Address Global Warming

Hamish McRae

By the time the Kyoto Protocol, the international treaty reducing the emissions of greenhouse gases, went into effect in February 2005, even its strongest supporters believed that the treaty would prove insufficient to completely solve the problem of global warming. In the following viewpoint Hamish McRae argues that even with its flaws, the Kyoto Protocol is an important first step in reducing greenhouse gas emissions. Although China and India were excluded from the new regulations, he claims, technology developed by the regulated countries will in time reduce emissions in China, India, and other developing nations. McRae is an economic journalist based in London, and the author of *The World in 2020: Power, Culture, and Prosperity.*

As you read, consider the following questions:

1. According to the viewpoint, how much of the industrial world's carbon emissions is the United States responsible for?
2. Why was it relatively easy for Russia to reduce its energy use, as the author explains?
3. How has Copenhagen combated global warming and become a "livable city," in the author's view?

After seven years, huge international debate and the freezing out of George [W.] Bush's United States from the international community, the Kyoto Protocol is formally ratified today [February 16, 2005].

The agreement, which seeks to limit the world's carbon emissions, was signed by 84 countries in Japan's former capital city in 1997. It bound the industrialised countries to cut emissions by 5 per cent from their 1990 level by 2012.

The treaty has been hailed as the key step forward in confronting the environmental challenges posed by climate change. But it remains controversial: is it a great leap forward in international co-operation or another example of empty political posturing? Or maybe, just maybe, something of both?

The case for cutting the global output of greenhouse gases is the link between such emissions and global warming—a link still unproven but for which there is strong circumstantial evidence. This is accepted by most industrialised nations.

The Treaty Is Ratified

But for the agreement to become international law two things had to happen. One was that 55 countries had to get it approved by their national legislatures. The other was that the countries approving it had to include a sufficient number of industrial countries to account for 55 per cent of their global emissions in 1990.

The first target was relatively easily met, but the "early signers" were largely small countries that did not use a lot of energy. The second was tougher, particularly since in March 2001, the new U.S. President, George Bush, said his country was not prepared to ratify the treaty. The U.S. unsurprisingly is the world's largest user of energy (and hence accounts for 36 per cent of carbon emissions of the industrial countries) so the second hurdle became harder to surmount. But last November [2004] Russia, which had previously indicated it would not sign up, switched sides. Russia has been a huge (and inefficient) user of energy and accounted for more than 17 per cent of global emissions in 1990. Suddenly the 55 per cent barrier was breached and the protocol could become law.

For many people this is a time for rejoicing, an example of international co-operation for a common good. Like the Montreal Protocol of 1987, which banned the production of CFCs [chlorofluorocarbons], it has demonstrated that countries were prepared to implement policies that might act against their short-term national self-interest in order to promote long-term global environmental aims. Countries that have refused to ratify Kyoto, most notably the U.S. and Australia, are duly pilloried. President Bush has been particularly singled out as a bad global citizen.

For others, this has been an exercise that at best is wishful thinking and at worst hypocrisy. Unlike the Montreal Protocol, which had a clear objective and clear benefits—reducing the damage to the ozone layer—Kyoto is both badly constructed and uncertain in its impact. And the countries that matter most have not signed up.

How should the thoughtful non-specialist respond to these conflicting perspectives? What we really want to know is whether in 20 or 30 years' time it will be seen as an important first step towards keeping the world a habitable place, or as a failed experiment, setting the wrong priorities and actually making future international co-operation more difficult to sustain. Perhaps the best way forward is to look at the criticisms of Kyoto and then see whether, despite those criticisms, it is still a useful process.

What About China and India?

Take first the argument that it is badly constructed and in particular that it excludes the country that is increasing its emissions fastest at the moment and which is now the second largest importer of oil: China. China is already the world's fifth or sixth-largest economy. It is growing at around 9 per cent a year and relies heavily on fossil fuels for powering this growth. Last year China installed as much new electricity generating capacity, mostly fossil fueled, as the entire electricity output of the UK.

And we have seen nothing yet. By the Kyoto target year of 2012 China will in all probability have become the world's third largest economy, behind only Japan and the U.S. Indeed were China not to have become the world's third-largest economy, everyone would be the worse for it as it would suggest some kind of political and economic collapse there, with all the misery that would entail.

Sack. © 2005 by the *Star Tribune*. Reproduced by permission of Knight Ridder/Tribune Information.

The other great global giant, India, is also increasing its energy use. Its economy has been growing at almost as fast a pace, around 7–8 per cent a year. Its energy use at the moment is much lower, for it has not experienced such rapid industrialisation and its building boom has been more muted. But it has become almost as large a car market as China, has the world's largest road-building programme and the spread of air-conditioning will ensure that its energy use continues to soar.

Kyoto Opens Debate

So does the exclusion of these two giants—and much of the rest of the developing world—destroy the rationale of Kyoto? It certainly weakens it. Our perspectives of economic power have changed radically since 1997. Maybe we should have realised that the new industrial countries would determine the world's energy demands and hence its carbon emissions and sought to bring them into the tent. But the debate within both China and India in some ways supports the Kyoto ideal, even if neither country is bound by it. Anyone who has been to China recently will be aware of the problem of air pollution with which the country is wrestling. Shanghai is beset with power shortages. Within China there is a serious debate as to how it can continue to grow at its present pace without being held back by environmental pressures.

In India much the same debate is happening, too. It is clear that India cannot follow the Chinese growth model, for its population pressure is even greater and its natural resources scarcer. So it has to find a way of growing by using energy more efficiently. In lots of small ways—taxis, for example, run on natural gas—it is seeking to improve its environment standards.

So it is very much in the self-interest of both China and India to expand their economies in the "greenest" way possible. But how? Both use technology developed in the rich world. If that technology becomes more efficient, cleaner, and less carbon-intensive, they will apply it. Insofar as the efforts to meet Kyoto standards drive Western Europe and Japan to develop better technology, that will inevitably improve the environmental performance of China, India, and other fast-growing developing countries.

So Kyoto helps China and India become cleaner, even though they are not bound by it.

A Controversy over Starting Points

What of the next criticism, that Kyoto does not fully reflect different countries' starting points? Well to some extent it does, as countries have been set different targets within the 5 per cent overall cut, so Switzerland has to cut its carbon output by 8 per cent while Australia increases its by the same amount. In addition, countries that take measures to absorb carbon, for example through reforestation, are allowed to unleash more of it. But the fundamental point does stand—it is easier for some countries to meet their targets than others.

For example, it is relatively easy for Russia to cut its energy use because in 1990 it had large and inefficient heavy industries that have now been shut down. And from a base of huge inefficiency, the first steps in cutting emissions are relatively easy—all you need do is to apply good practice developed elsewhere. Rationally you can argue that the Kyoto accord is not in Russia's self-interest, as not only would it benefit from a slightly warmer—and therefore more prosperous—Siberia, but as an exporter of oil and gas it would gain from the continuing energy profligacy of its main customer, Western Europe.

And yet, signing up costs Russia nothing. Russian membership of the club will not significantly affect global carbon emissions, but brings political benefits. It can present itself as a virtuous friend of the EU [European Union] and of the international community—unlike the U.S.

Targets Ignore Important Factors

A further point is that the targets do not fully reflect differences of population growth or economic success. For example, they do not take into account a shrinking population in Germany and a rising one in the U.S., nor Germany's economic stagnation or America's boom. When Kyoto was negotiated it was thought the fall in Germany's population would not begin until well past 2012. As things have turned out, it started last year [in 2004]. Meanwhile, America's population growth has run ahead of forecasts. Similar differences in economic performance were not expected either—and it would be hard to defend Kyoto if it became a way of punishing economic success.

But it should not become that. You can acknowledge that it is crude, despite the tweaks to try to make it less so. You can acknowledge that the information on which the original deal was based was flawed. But you can still believe that it nudges countries in the right direction rather than the wrong one.

Energy prices look likely to remain high for a generation. Countries that can grow—both in population and in living standards—without stretching energy supplies will find it easier to make progress than those that can't, so the agreement pushes countries towards policies that are, in general, in their self-interest. A U.S. that had a more efficient car fleet now would be richer, for it would be better able to withstand high oil prices. Living standards would be higher and the dollar would be higher, for it would be less dependent on oil imports. Strategically too, it would be more secure.

The Start of a New Era

For over a decade, more than 100 countries have strategized how to cut emissions of greenhouse gases. The activation of the Kyoto Protocol on February 16 [2005] marks the start of a new era and an unprecedented worldwide endeavor—both competitive and cooperative—to place the world's first binding caps on global warming pollution.

"For years there's been talk about the need to give countries and companies a market signal to start cutting global warming pollution while driving economic growth forward," said Environmental Defense international counsel Annie Petsonk. "That signal is the starting bell for the Kyoto Protocol's emissions trading market, which will launch real cuts in global warming pollution around the world while stimulating new technologies with huge potential for creating jobs in cleaner energy and more sustainable agriculture."

Environmental Defense, "World Starts Counting Carbs to Tackle Global Warming," www.undoit.org, February 16, 2005.

Beyond economics there is such a thing as politics. Democracies have to work with the grain of public opinion. A Russian president can force through legislation in the way a U.S. one cannot. Criticism of the U.S. has to be tempered with an acknowledgment of the will of its people. Arguably by immediately acknowledging that Kyoto would never be passed by Congress, the present President was at least being more honest than his predecessor, who sidelined political debate on the matter until he was out of office.

Yet here again, while acknowledging the separation of powers in the U.S. it is surely possible also to acknowledge the power of persuasion. There is a significant minority within the U.S. that seeks to reduce environmental damage caused by high energy use. The fashionable car for Hollywood stars is the hybrid Toyota Prius, which does more than 50mpg [miles per gallon]. America can look to places such as Copenhagen [the capital of Denmark], which has over 20 years sought to get people out of cars and on to bikes and public transport—and has created a much more livable city than similar U.S. cities. So politics can lead as well as follow and environmentalism feels modern in a way that profligate energy use does not.

Is Kyoto Our Highest Priority?

There is one final line of criticism of Kyoto that needs to be acknowledged: that it is not the highest priority. Other aims, such as the elimination of malaria or combating AIDS in Africa, have greater claims on scarce resources. The Danish statistician Bjorn Lomborg has controversially argued that Kyoto slows the growth of emissions by an insignificant amount at a very high cost. While it is certainly desirable to do so, it would be better to put resources into the development of alternative energy and tackling the effects of global warming.

These objections need to be taken seriously. Economic resources—just like fossil fuels—are finite and they need to be directed where they will be most effective. Money spent on wind farms is money not available for drugs in Africa. But the best response to this, surely, is to see Kyoto as an early and imperfect step along a long and difficult road.

Its huge benefit is to focus attention on a global problem— and a global problem that the market cannot fix. The costs of global climate change are very long term and most uncertain. The markets can match supply and demand today but their focus is inevitably short-term. They find it hard to look 30 years out. And there are external costs—felt beyond the countries that produce and consume energy—that are carried by the world as a whole. That is why the world, or much of it, signed up to Kyoto and it is why we should celebrate today.

What matters most, though, is what happens next. Somewhere out in the future is the next generation of technologies that will wean the world off fossil fuels and provide it with renewable power. But we cannot see those clearly so meanwhile we have to be careful with what we have got.

If Kyoto encourages the hunt for the new technologies— as it has—that is worth something. If it makes us think a little more about our own use of energy that is worth something too. If it is the start of a wider global process of cooperation in conservation, then it is worth a huge amount. A good day for the world.

> *"The urgent tasks of a serious climate-change policy are scientific, technological, and institutional—and these can only be distorted and undermined by a precipitate move toward controls [like Kyoto]."*

The Kyoto Protocol Cannot Address Global Warming

Christopher DeMuth

When the United States withdrew from the Kyoto Protocol discussions in 2001, many expected the treaty to collapse. In the following viewpoint Christopher DeMuth argues that this collapse was both inevitable and welcome, because the Kyoto Protocol was based on emotion and politics rather than on science and technology. He contends that the Kyoto Protocol was a flawed short-term solution to a problem that requires long-term planning. Despite predictions, the protocol went into effect in 2005. DeMuth is president of the American Enterprise Institute for Public Policy Research, a conservative think tank.

As you read, consider the following questions:

1. According to DeMuth, when might we begin to see effects of substantial global warming?
2. Instead of focusing on controls, as called for by the Kyoto Protocol, what should the climate change agenda focus on, according to the author?
3. What date would have been the baseline against which each nation's reductions in emissions would be measured, as reported by the author?

Christopher DeMuth, "The Kyoto Treaty Deserved to Die," *Energy Crunch*, September 2001. Copyright © 2001 by the American Enterprise Institute for Public Policy Research. Reproduced with permission of *The American Enterprise*, a magazine of Politics, Business, and Culture. On the web at www.TAEmag.com.

President [George W.] Bush's firm rejection of the Kyoto Protocol on Climate Change put the final nail in the coffin of a doomed project. By 2012, the agreement would have required the leading industrial nations to reduce their "greenhouse gas" emissions to levels below *1990* totals (regardless of population growth and economic transformations in the various countries), and would have exempted China and other developing nations entirely (despite the fact that their growing emissions would have swamped the reductions from the developed nations). Long before President Bush acted, this approach had been rejected by the U.S. Senate in a vote of 95–0, which is why President [Bill] Clinton never submitted the treaty for ratification. Nor had any other major nation adopted the agreement when implementation negotiations collapsed amidst acrimony and name-calling in November 2000.[1]

The failure of the Kyoto Protocol was both inevitable and desirable—inevitable because it required the impossible, desirable because it stood in the way of feasible, effective climate-change policies. Those who framed the agreement treated global warming as a well-understood, immediate problem—indeed as an incipient crisis. This view produced a program of drastic short-term controls on emissions of CO_2 and other gases, which in turn produced irresoluble economic conflicts, both among the developed nations that negotiated the agreement and between the developed and developing nations.

The key features of the climate-change debate are large degrees of uncertainty and a long time horizon. Although it is fairly well-established that the Earth's atmosphere has warmed somewhat (one degree Fahrenheit) during the past century, it's not clear why this happened. The warming may have been due to human impositions (the burning of fossil fuels and other incidents of industrial growth), or to natural solar or climate variations, or to some of each. Whatever the causes, we don't know if future warming trends will be large or small, or whether the net environmental and economic

---

1. In February 2005 the Kyoto Protocol went into effect, having obtained support from enough countries. The U.S. did not sign the treaty.

consequences (including both beneficial and harmful effects) may be large or small.

These uncertainties are carefully described in the recent official reports on global warming—the National Academy of Sciences' June 2001 report to President Bush, and the earlier *Third Assessment Report of the Intergovernmental Panel on Climate Change* (IPCC). It is regrettable that the media accounts of these studies have downplayed or ignored the uncertainties, for they are fundamental to the question of right policy, not academic quibbles or excuses for delay. Equally fundamental is the long time horizon: Even if we are in for substantial warming, the effects will not begin to occur for several decades, probably at least a half century.

We Need More Time

It is important to appreciate that we have time, because we *need* time, and not only to get a better grip on causes and consequences. Regulating CO_2 emissions on a global scale would require political institutions that do not now exist—and, in the developing nations, political support that will not exist until their citizens have attained significantly higher standards of living. Moreover, the progressive replacement over time of fossil-fuel-burning by newer methods of producing energy may solve the problem without recourse to controls. If policy encouragement is needed, existing and prospective pollution controls may be sufficient. Finally, human and ecological adaption, and even direct climate "bio-engineering," could be equally or more effective responses to harmful warming whatever the cause—and would be the *only* effective responses to natural warming.

We will know vastly more about the relative merits of these alternatives several decades from now. And we will almost certainly be vastly richer—a key consideration, especially in China and other currently poor nations, if the best responses involve taxes, regulatory controls, or public expenditures that impinge seriously on economic growth. As economist Thomas Schelling has noted, the speed at which we move toward acceptable atmospheric concentrations of greenhouse gases makes little difference as a climatic matter, but a tremendous difference as an economic matter.

The collapse of the Kyoto negotiations in the fall of 2000, and the Bush administration's renunciation of the agreement in the spring of 2001, have produced a great deal of recrimination, finger-pointing, and political posturing. But problems that are new, complex, and unfamiliar often prompt a succession of false starts before an effective approach is hit upon. That the first stab at global-climate policy was a failure should be no more surprising or dispiriting than the failure of initial attempts to alleviate the Great Depression, or to counter the spread of communism.

Shelton. © 2005 by King Features Syndicate. Reproduced by permission.

The Kyoto failure suggests a new, three-part approach to the problem. The first two parts are a variant on the New Age slogan, "Think Globally, Act Locally." Vastly more serious, de-politicized scientific research needs to be devoted to the global aspects of climate change; but immediate government actions should be local, regional, and incremental rather than international. The third part of any immediate program should be a moratorium on regulatory controls for the time being. Premature emissions controls or energy

185

taxes will only transform the climate-change issue from one concerned with cause, consequence, and best-response to one concerned with political and economic advantage.

Think Globally

Global climate variation is an immensely complicated matter, and needs to be thought through much more systematically. The major effect of new knowledge accumulated over the last decade has actually been *increased uncertainty* concerning likely future warming and its consequences (compared to what many observers *thought* they knew). Now that the hasty turn to draconian regulatory controls, as envisioned in Kyoto, has reached a dead-end, the climate-change agenda should shift instead to scientific research, technology development, and institution building.

The U.S. government currently spends about $1.7 billion annually on climate-change research. More than $1 billion of it is NASA [National Aeronautics and Space Administration] expenditures, mainly on satellite weather monitoring. Only a few hundred million is for all other aspects of climate science, for developing alternative responses to warming, and for investigating non-fossil-fuel energy technologies. This is a truly piddling sum relative to the size of the issue, and reflects the Clinton administration's adamant uninterest in climate-change science. "Science has spoken," pronounced former Vice President [Al] Gore: For him, science was a source of authority, and a weapon with which to browbeat and silence political critics, rather than a discovery process driven by skepticism and falsification. At the early stages of a research project, "solid science" is not solid at all but consists of open competition among multiple hypotheses. Reversing the closed-minded legacy of the Clinton years is now a matter of some urgency.

Treasury Secretary Paul O'Neill, when he was CEO of [the aluminum corporation] Alcoa, recommended a large increase in expenditures on all facets of climate-change science, and the commissioning of an independent board of respected academic, professional, and business leaders to oversee the research and issue periodic reports synthesizing the state of knowledge. President Bush's recent statement on climate change, with its mention of a Climate Change Research Initiative and a Climate Change Technology Initiative, appears to contemplate a substantial expansion and reordering of federal efforts, although the specifics are still being developed.

The current research effort could be improved in many ways other than just spending more. Many top scientists believe that the U.S. research program (like the international IPCC program—which has tended to ignore many distinguished physicists and meteorologists whose work casts doubt on the influence of greenhouse gases on global temperature trends) is skewed toward scientists who take an alarmist view of the problem. A competition of ideas, including iconoclastic views, needs to be encouraged rather than suppressed. The research effort should encompass not only climate-change causation and forecasting and non-fossil-fuel energy technologies, but also adaptive and "geoengineering" strategies for responding to potential harmful warming from whatever source (including natural variation). The United States should continue to take an active role in the IPCC but take steps to de-politicize its functioning.

Act Locally

The Kyoto Protocol's controls over CO_2 and other emissions would have begun in 2008 and included a complex scheme of trading in emissions "credits" across national boundaries. It was fantasy to think that such a scheme, involving scores of countries, could have been put in place in less time than it takes a single city to get organized for an Olympic Games. Even the advanced nations lack sufficient information on emissions and "sinks" (such as forests, which *absorb* large quantities of CO_2 from the atmosphere) to permit trading in credits for reducing emissions. And many poorer nations are just too deficient in their legal and political institutions to take part at all in such complex efforts.

In the early 1990s, several delegations of officials from the Russian and Chinese governments visited the United States to study how to establish securities exchanges in their countries. They learned, to their dismay, that the first step was not to design a trading floor or computer software or communications networks, but rather to establish honest and accurate systems of financial accounting and disclosure, so that securities could be priced and traded with confidence. In global emissions trading, the accounting systems have only begun to be established.

Kyoto Protocol Will Have Little Effect

Kyoto temperature effect: year 2100

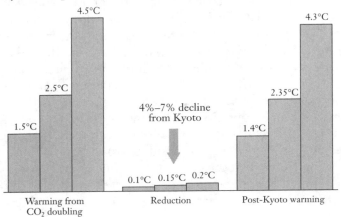

Warming from CO₂ doubling: 1.5°C, 2.5°C, 4.5°C

Reduction (4%–7% decline from Kyoto): 0.1°C, 0.15°C, 0.2°C

Post-Kyoto warming: 1.4°C, 2.35°C, 4.3°C

Tom M.L. Wigley, *Geophysical Research Letters*, July 1, 1998.

If controls on CO_2 and other greenhouse gases turn out to be necessary, much work needs to be done to build the institutions appropriate to the task. Kyoto teaches that it is impractical to try to build them everywhere all at once; a major cause of its collapse was the differing interests of the economically developed and undeveloped nations, and the complexity of establishing institutions for carbon trading that will work with differing political systems. A more modest, incremental approach to institution building is called for, involving smaller groups of nations joined by geographic proximity or economic interest.

One excellent start would be for the United States, Canada, and Mexico to work together to build reliable national inventories of greenhouse gas emissions and sinks, and to develop model institutions for cross-border trading of emissions credits. Such a project would be much more likely to produce useful information and tangible institutional progress than anything attempted under Kyoto. The United States and its two neighbors feature significant variations in natural resources, industrialization, GDP [gross domestic product], culture, and political institutions, yet they already work productively together on a variety of problems. Their three heads of state—the "three amigos"—are looking for new joint projects. Asian and European nations, which have been so critical of the U.S. withdrawal from Kyoto, should be invited to launch similar regional projects.

There are numerous other opportunities for immediate cooperative projects. Japanese industry has been successful in developing alternative energy technologies like hybrid gas-electric automobiles, as well as promising methods for recycling CO_2 emissions back into industrial processes. The new [Prime Minister Junichiro] Koizumi government is searching eagerly for projects to demonstrate its dedication to the global environmental improvement. A joint U.S.-Japan project on alternative energy technologies and CO_2 recycling would no doubt suffer from the shortcomings of all such government projects, but it would involve work where the two nations have unique assets (advanced science and technology) and common interests going beyond the global warming issue (such as achieving greater energy independence).

Localized projects such as these would be the undertakings of economically advanced nations, which is appropriate. The poorer nations face many more urgent problems than the prospect of warmer weather 50 years or a century from now. It is the rich, high-tech, environmentally concerned nations that should be working on the climate-change problem. Eventually they may be able to help later-developing nations bypass the fossil-fuel era in energy production, just as many of them are now bypassing the copper-wire era in telecommunications.

No Quick Regulatory Controls

The impossibility of establishing a global emissions control program in a short period of time was only a secondary cause of Kyoto's collapse; the primary cause was the enormous *cost* of the controls and the unequal and arbitrary distribution of costs within and between nations. Part of the problem was the Protocol's odd requirement that each nation's reductions were to be measured against its emissions at a much earlier date—1990. This would have produced bizarre anomalies. The Russian government, for instance, would have been eligible for hundreds of billions of dollars' worth of "credits" for reducing its emissions, simply because Russian industry collapsed in the 1990s. And the "baseline" issue was only one of numerous features of Kyoto's CO_2 control-and-trading program that caused the negotiations to degenerate into a scramble for economic advantage. The almost comical denouement came when the European nations insisted on *weakening* the control program to make it work more to the economic disadvantage of the United States.

The moment climate-change policy turns to the issue of emissions controls, it ceases to be about science and starts to be about economic interests. That is the most important lesson of the Kyoto collapse. But in this case it was only an accident that the forces of economic interest ended up scuttling a bad agreement rather than securing it (as has happened more than once in domestic environmental policy).

The day may come when the science of global warming has gelled to the extent that hard and contentious choices about a costly control regime must be faced. But that day is decades away at worst, and it may not come at all. If it does come, the interest-group pressures will be less serious than today—because our knowledge of the nature of the problem and appropriate remedies will be much more confident. For the time being, the urgent tasks of a serious climate-change policy are scientific, technological, and institutional—and these can only be distorted and undermined by a precipitate move toward controls.

Periodical Bibliography

The following articles have been selected to supplement the diverse views presented in this chapter.

Robert U. Ayres — "How Economists Have Misjudged Global Warming," *World Watch*, September/October 2001.

Seth Borenstein — "Scientists: Bush Administration Needs Plan to Tackle Global Warming," *Knight Ridder/Tribune News Service*, July 24, 2003.

Stephanie Cohen — "Energy Dreams and Energy Realities," *New Atlantis*, Spring 2004.

James Hansen — "A Common-Sense Solution to Global Warming," *New Perspectives Quarterly*, Winter 2001.

James Hansen — "Defusing the Global Warming Time Bomb," *Scientific American*, March 2004.

Elizabeth Kolbert — "Annals of Science: The Climate of Man," *New Yorker*, April 25, 2005; May 2, 2005; May 9, 2005.

Bill McKibben — "Sins of Emission," *Sojourners*, March 2004.

Iain Murray — "Global Warming Not a Cost-Effective Target," *Atlanta Journal Constitution*, October 4, 2004.

Kim Oksana — "The Kyoto Protocol: Universal Concern for Climate Change," *UN Chronicle*, September/November 2004.

Daniel Sarewitz and Roger Pielke Jr. — "Breaking the Global Warming Gridlock," *Atlantic Monthly*, July 2000.

Janet Sawin — "Long-Range Forecast," *World Watch*, March/April 2003.

Peter Schwartz and Spencer Reiss — "Nuclear Now: How Clean, Green Atomic Energy Can Stop Global Warming," *Wired*, February 2005.

Robert Socolow et al. — "Solving the Climate Problem: Technologies Available to Curb CO_2 Emissions," *Environment*, December 2004.

Robert N. Stavins — "Forging a More Effective Global Climate Treaty," *Environment*, December 2004.

Jerry Taylor — "Not Cheap, Not Green," *Washington Times*, August 4, 2003.

Dan Whipple — "Climate: Will Kyoto Leave the U.S. Behind?" *UPI Perspectives*, February 21, 2005.

For Further Discussion

Chapter 1

1. Geoffrey Lean and John F. McManus both use strong language in their viewpoints, writing of "disaster," "alarms," "danger," "control of fellow man," "drive for power," and "enchaining the planet." How does this type of language affect the way you respond to their arguments?

2. Based on the viewpoints in this chapter, how do you judge the current state of scientific knowledge about global warming? Do you accept Naomi Oreskes's claim that there is a scientific consensus, or do you find that there is still significant uncertainty in the scientific community? Explain.

3. Naomi Oreskes is a history professor whose research is in the history of scientific thought. The Greening Earth Society is a group sponsored by electric companies and their suppliers. Does this information affect how you evaluate their viewpoints? Why or why not?

Chapter 2

1. Thomas R. Karl and Kevin E. Trenberth contend that human activities cause global warming. William M. Gray argues that global warming is caused by natural fluctuations. On what aspects of climate and climate change do the two viewpoints agree? What is the central point of their disagreement?

2. The Sierra Club argues that sport utility vehicles emit more greenhouse gases than do other cars, while Sal Rosken points out that the total emissions from such vehicles is small when considering other influences on global climate. Is it sensible to ask individuals to stop driving SUVs, even if their sacrifice might make only a small difference in the environment? Use the viewpoints to support your answer.

Chapter 3

1. Charles W. Petit presents the melting of polar ice as evidence of dramatic climate change. What evidence does he give that global warming is the cause? Jens Bischof writes that no one knows what is causing the ice to melt, and those who claim global warming is to blame are seeing only what they expect to see. Is he persuasive? Why?

2. Ross Gelbspan and Dennis Avery write about benefits and harms in their viewpoints. As Avery explains it, how will global warming help humans? As Gelbspan explains it, how will hu-

mans be harmed? Could both authors be right? Use evidence from the viewpoints to explain your answer.

Chapter 4

1. Fred Krupp's viewpoint argues that Americans will have to make sacrifices in order to solve the global warming problem. What strategies does he use to make these sacrifices appear more acceptable? How does he appeal to American patriotism in order to win people to his side? Does Sallie Baliunas make any similar appeals to patriotic feeling?

2. William Kovacs contends that the technology to reduce carbon dioxide simply does not exist. If he is correct, how does this affect your reading of Fred Krupp's or Sallie Baliunas's viewpoints? Use examples from the text to explain your answer.

3. Lester R. Brown, Jerry Taylor and Peter VanDoren, John McCain, and the coalition of environmental groups all agree that the world will need to find alternatives to carbon-emitting fuels. What else do they agree on?

4. John McCain argues that nuclear power is the only alternative source of power that could replace fossil fuels quickly enough to make a difference in global warming. The coalition of environmental groups argues that nuclear power is too dangerous to adopt widely. Could both be right? Use evidence from the viewpoints to support your answer.

5. Lester R. Brown and Jerry Taylor and Peter VanDoren discuss government subsidies. Brown argues that subsidies of fossil fuels gives them an unfair pricing advantage over renewable energy, while Taylor and VanDoren claim that subsidies of renewables has artificially lowered their prices. What are some of the reasons that a government might choose to give financial support to energy companies? What should a government consider in deciding which types of energy to support?

6. An issue touched on by several of the viewpoints in this chapter is the differences between a country's responsibilities to its own citizens and its responsibilities to the world at large. Alternative energies, for example, could potentially make the world a better place for everyone, but they would definitely be more expensive for the consumers who use them. How should a nation's policy makers weigh such gains and losses?

Organizations to Contact

aBetterEarth.org
Institute for Humane Studies, George Mason University
3301 North Fairfax Dr., Suite 440, Arlington, VA 22201
(800) 697-8799 • fax: (703) 993-4890
e-mail: info@abetterearth.org • Web site: www.abetterearth.org
aBetterEarth.org is a project of the Institute for Humane Studies
at George Mason University, a nonprofit educational organization
that promotes innovative thinking about how a world that is
peaceful, prosperous, and free can be achieved. Its goal is to encourage students to think critically about the successes and failures
of the environmental movement. The project sponsors a Web site,
a summer seminar, and an e-mail newsletter.

Competitive Enterprise Institute (CEI)
1001 Connecticut Ave. NW, Suite 1250, Washington, DC 20036
(202) 331-1010 • fax: (202) 331-0640
e-mail: info@cei.org • Web site: www.cei.org
The Competitive Enterprise Institute, founded in 1984, is a nonprofit public policy organization dedicated to advancing the prin-
ciples of free enterprise and limited government. CEI argues that
the best solutions to environmental problems come from individuals making their own choices in a free marketplace. It publishes
opinion and analysis pieces on its online *EnviroWire* and an online
Daily Update, and sponsors the Cooler Heads Project.

The Energy Information Administration (EIA)
1000 Independence Ave. SW, Washington, DC 20585
(202) 586-8800
e-mail: infoctr@eia.doe.gov • Web site: http://eia.doe.gov
The Energy Information Administration, created by Congress in
1977, is a statistical agency of the U.S. Department of Energy. It provides data, forecasts, and analyses to promote sound policy making,
efficient markets, and public understanding of energy issues. EIA's
online offerings include a "Kid's Page," an "Ask an Expert" link, reports of annual data going back to 1949, and projections to 2025.

Environmental Defense

Membership and Public Information
1875 Connecticut Ave. NW, Suite 600, Washington, DC 20009
(800) 684-3322
e-mail: members@environmentaldefense.org
Web site: www.environmentaldefense.org

Environmental Defense, founded in 1967, works to protect the environmental rights of all people, including future generations, low-income communities, and communities of color. It focuses on U.S. environmental problems and the U.S. role in causing and solving environmental problems. Environmental Defense maintains an online archive of its articles, reports, press releases, and fact sheets, as well as resources for educators.

Global Climate Coalition (GCC)

1275 K St. NW, Washington, DC 20005
(202) 682-9161
Web site: www.globalclimate.org

The Global Climate Coalition is an organization of trade associations established in 1989 to be a voice for business in the global warming debate. GCC sends representatives to all international climate change negotiations. The organization publishes occasional position papers, available on its Web site.

Global Warming Information Center

The National Center for Public Policy Research
501 Capitol Ct. NE, Washington, DC 20002
(202) 543-4110 • fax: (202) 543-5975
e-mail: info@nationalcenter.org
Web site: www.nationalcenter.org

The Global Warming Information Center is a project of the John P. McGovern M.D. Center for Environmental and Regulatory Affairs of the National Center for Public Policy Research, which supports strong national defense and free markets. It collects on its Web site various articles and transcripts of testimony that promote the belief that private owners, rather than governments, are the best stewards of the environment. There is also a "Facts on Global Warming" link to other collections of skeptical articles and documents.

Greening Earth Society

333 John Carlyle St., Suite 530, Alexandria, VA 22314
(800) 529-4503 • fax: (703) 684-9297
e-mail: info@co2andclimate.org
Web site: www.co2andclimate.org

The Greening Earth Society is a nonprofit organization of rural electric cooperatives and municipal electric utilities, their fuel suppliers, and individuals. It expresses scientific skepticism about the potential for catastrophic climate change due to human-caused carbon dioxide emissions. The society sponsors a Web site, *CO₂ & Climate*, to provide information about the effects of carbon dioxide on the atmosphere, and it publishes periodic world climate alerts.

Greenpeace

702 H St. NW, Washington, DC 20001
(800) 326-0959
e-mail: info@wdc.greenpeace.org
Web site: www.greenpeace.org

Greenpeace is an international nonprofit organization. Founded in 1971, it focuses on worldwide threats to the planet's biodiversity and environment, and directs attention to its mission through public acts of nonviolent civil disobedience. Greenpeace publishes technical reports, including "All Emission, No Solution: Energy Hypocrisy and the Asian Development Bank in Southeast Asia" and "Background Briefing on Climate Litigation."

Intergovernmental Panel on Climate Change (IPCC)

c/o World Meteorological Organization
7bis Ave. de la Paix, CP 2300, CH-1211 Geneva 2, Switzerland
Web site: www.ipcc.ch

The IPCC was established by the United Nations to assess scientific, technical, and socioeconomic information relevant for the understanding of climate change. In addition to the *IPCC Third Assessment Report—Climate Change 2001*, it publishes reports of expert meetings and workshops, and methodology reports including *IPCC Report on Good Practice Guidance for Land Use, Land-Use Change and Forestry* and *Good Practice Guidance and Uncertainty Management in National Greenhouse Gas Inventories*.

National Environmental Trust

1200 Eighteenth St. NW, Fifth Floor, Washington, DC 20036
(202) 887-8800 • fax: (202) 887-8877
e-mail: info@net.org • Web site: www.net.org

The National Environmental Trust is a nonprofit, nonpartisan organization established in 1994 to inform citizens about environmental problems and how they affect human health and quality of life. Its educational programs focus on clean air, global warming, energy, and other issues. NET publishes reports, fact sheets, and press releases.

National Oceanic and Atmospheric Administration (NOAA) Paleoclimatology Program

325 Broadway St., Boulder, CO 80305-3328
(303) 497-6280 • fax: (303) 497-6513
e-mail: paleo@noaa.gov • Web site: www.ncdc.noaa.gov

The NOAA Paleoclimatology Program researches the patterns, processes, and causes of past climate variability, with the goal of improving the ability to predict future climate change. The program collects and publishes climate data from thousands of locations worldwide, and offers data, reports, and a discussion list on its Web site.

National Resources Defense Council (NRDC)

40 W. Twentieth St., New York, NY 10011
(212) 727-2700 • fax: (212) 727-1773
e-mail: nrdcinfo@nrdc.org • Web site: www.nrdc.org

NRDC is an environmental action organization that works to support pro-environmental legislation and defeat anti-environment legislation. Specifically, it calls on government to work with its citizens to reduce pollution, protect endangered species, and create a sustainable way of life for humankind. NRDC publishes a quarterly magazine, *OnEarth*, and e-mail bulletins including *Earth Action*, *Legislative Watch*, and *This Green Life*.

New Hope Environmental Services

5 Boar's Head Ln., Charlottesville, VA 22903
(434) 295-7462 • fax: (434) 295-7549
e-mail: info@nhes.com • Web site: www.nhes.com

New Hope Environmental Services, established in 1994, is an advocacy science consulting firm that produces research and commentary on the nature of climate, climate change, and U.S. and international environmental policy. Its scientists, analysts, and editors conduct and publish research for private companies and for the public. In addition to articles in scientific journals, New Hope publishes a biweekly online periodical, *World Climate Report*, presenting scientific evidence concluding that warnings about climate change are exaggerated.

Pew Center on Global Climate Change
2101 Wilson Blvd., Suite 550, Arlington, VA 22201
(703) 516-4146 • fax: (703) 841-1422
Web site: www.pewclimate.org

The Pew Center on Global Climate Change is a research group made up of business leaders, policy makers, scientists, and other experts. It produces reports on protecting climate while sustaining economic growth; these reports are distributed to opinion leaders throughout the world and are available for free download. Recent titles include *Comparison of Passenger Vehicle Fuel Economy and Greenhouse Gas Standards Around the World* and *Observed Impacts of Climate Change in the U.S.*

Safe Climate for Business
World Resources Institute
10 G St. NE, Washington, DC 20002
(202) 729-7600 • fax: (202) 729-7610
e-mail: info@safeclimate.net • Web site: www.safeclimate.net

Safe Climate for Business is a joint project of the World Resources Institute and the Center for Environmental Leadership in Business, dedicated to helping business of all sizes understand and take action on climate change. It seeks profitable solutions to environmental challenges. Its Web site offers articles about understanding climate change, evaluating emissions, and solutions for reducing climate impact. World Resources Institute publishes an annual *CO_2 Inventory Report*.

The Science and Environmental Policy Project (SEPP)
1600 South Eads St., Suite 712-S, Arlington, VA 22202-2907
(703) 920-2744
e-mail: comments@sepp.org • Web site: www.sepp.org

The Science and Environmental Policy Project is an educational organization founded in 1990 by S. Fred Singer, professor emeritus of environmental science at the University of Virginia, to present the scientific case against the theory of global warming and against the Kyoto Protocol. SEPP's Web site maintains an archive of older speeches, reports, and press releases about climate change, and a "New on the SEPP Web" section with recent articles. SEPP publishes a weekly online newsletter, the *Week That Was*.

Union of Concerned Scientists (UCS)
2 Brattle Square, Cambridge, MA 02238-9105
(617) 547-5552 • fax: (617) 864-9405
Web site: www.ucsusa.org

Union of Concerned Scientists is an independent, nonprofit alliance of concerned citizens and scientists. It was founded in 1969 by faculty members and students at the Massachusetts Institute of Technology, who were concerned about the misuse of science and technology in society. It sponsors the Sound Science Initiative, through which scientists provide information on environmental science to government and the media. UCS publishes an annual report, and posts on its Web site information about global environment, clean vehicles, clean energy, and other issues.

U.S. Global Change Research Program (USGCRP)
1717 Pennsylvania Ave. NW, Suite 250, Washington, DC 20006
(202) 223-6262 • fax: (202) 223-3065
e-mail: information@usgcrp.gov • Web site: www.usgcrp.gov

The USGCRP supports research on the interactions of natural and human-induced changes in the global environment and their implications for society. Its participants include representatives of several government agencies. It publishes an annual report, *Our Changing Planet*, which generally accompanies the president's annual budget.

Worldwatch Institute
1776 Massachusetts Ave. NW, Washington, DC 20036-1904
(202) 452-1999 • fax: (202) 296-7365
e-mail: worldwatch@worldwatch.org
Web site: www.worldwatch.org

Worldwatch Institute is a research institution that analyzes and focuses attention on global problems, including environmental issues such as global warming, and the relationship between trade and the environment. It publishes annual book-length reports, *State of the World* and *Vital Signs*, the bimonthly *World Watch* magazine, and a series of *Worldwatch Papers* on current environmental topics.

Bibliography of Books

Jonathan Adler et al.
Greenhouse Policy Without Regrets: A Free Market Approach to the Uncertain Risks of Climate Change. Washington, DC: Competitive Enterprise Institute, 2000.

Tom Athanasiou and Paul Baer
Dead Heat: Global Justice and Global Warming. New York: Seven Stories Press, 2002.

Wilfred Beckerman
A Poverty of Reason: Sustainable Development and Economic Growth. Oakland, CA: Independent Institute, 2003.

Jens Bischof
Ice Drift, Ocean Circulation, and Climate Change. New York: Springer, 2001.

Lester R. Brown
Plan B: Rescuing a Planet Under Stress and a Civilization in Trouble. Washington, DC: Earth Policy Institute, 2003.

Michael Crichton
State of Fear. New York: HarperCollins, 2004.

Guy Dauncey
Stormy Weather: 101 Solutions to Climate Change. Gabriola Island, BC: New Society Publishers, 2001.

John M. Deutch and Richard K. Lester
Making Technology Work: Applications in Energy and the Environment. New York: Cambridge University Press, 2004.

Pete Domenici, Blythe Lyons, and Julian J. Steyn
A Brighter Tomorrow: Fulfilling the Promise of Nuclear Energy. Lanham, MD: Rowman & Littlefield, 2004.

Brian Fagan
The Little Ice Age: How Climate Made History, 1300–1850. New York: Basic Books, 2000.

Ross Gelbspan
Boiling Point: How Politicians, Big Oil and Coal, Journalists, and Activists Have Fueled the Climate Crisis—and What We Can Do to Avert Disaster. New York: Basic Books, 2004.

Ross Gelbspan
The Heat Is On: The Climate Crisis, the Cover-Up, the Prescription. Cambridge, MA: Perseus, 1998.

Howard S. Geller
Energy Revolution: Policies for a Sustainable Future. Washington, DC: Island Press, 2003.

Al Gore
Earth in the Balance: Ecology and the Human Spirit. Boston: Houghton Mifflin, 1992.

Richard Heinberg
Powerdown: Options and Actions for a Post-Carbon World. Gabriola Island, BC: New Society Publishers, 2004.

John Houghton — *Global Warming, the Complete Briefing.* 3rd edition. Cambridge, UK: Cambridge University Press, 2004.

Robert Hunter — *Thermageddon: Countdown to 2030.* New York: Arcade, 2003.

Bjorn Lomborg — *The Skeptical Environmentalist.* Cambridge, UK: Cambridge University Press, 2002.

Mark Lynas — *High Tide: The Truth About Our Climate Crisis.* New York: Picador, 2004.

Doug Macdougall — *Frozen Earth: The Once and Future Story of Ice Ages.* Berkeley: University of California Press, 2004.

James J. McCarthy, ed. et al. — *Climate Change 2001: Impacts, Adaptation, and Vulnerability.* Cambridge, UK: Cambridge University Press, 2001.

Bill McGuire, Ian Mason, and Christopher Kilburn — *Natural Hazards and Environmental Change.* London: Arnold, 2002.

Aubrey Meyer — *Contraction and Convergence: The Global Solution to Climate Change.* Schumacher Briefing No. 5. Devon, UK: Green Books, 2000.

Patrick J. Michaels — *Meltdown: The Predictable Distortion of Global Warming by Scientists, Politicians, and the Media.* Washington, DC: Cato Institute, 2004.

Patrick J. Michaels and Robert C. Balling Jr. — *The Satanic Gases: Clearing the Air About Global Warming.* Washington, DC: Cato Institute, 2000.

Thomas G. Moore — *Climate of Fear: Why We Shouldn't Worry About Global Warming.* Washington, DC: Cato Institute, 1998.

National Academy of Sciences, Committee on the Science of Climate Change — *Climate Change Science: An Analysis of Some Key Questions.* Washington, DC: National Academies Press, 2001.

National Coal Council — *Coal Related Greenhouse Gas Management Issues.* Washington, DC: National Coal Council, 2003.

National Research Council — *Abrupt Climate Change: Inevitable Surprises.* Washington, DC: National Academy Press, 2002.

Fred Pearce — *Global Warming.* New York: DK Publishing, 2002.

S. George Philander — *Is the Temperature Rising? The Uncertain Science of Global Warming.* Princeton, NJ: Princeton University Press, 1998.

Laurence P. Pringle	*Global Warming: The Threat of Earth's Changing Climate.* New York: SeaStar Books, 2001.
Sir Martin Rees	*Our Final Hour: A Scientist's Warning.* New York: Basic Books, 2003.
Joseph J. Romm	*The Hype About Hydrogen: Fact and Fiction in the Race to Save the Climate.* Washington, DC: Island Press, 2004.
Terry Root and Stephen H. Schneider, eds.	*Wildlife Responses to Climate Changes.* Washington, DC: Island Press, 2002.
Janet L. Sawin	*Mainstreaming Renewable Energy in the 21st Century.* Washington, DC: Worldwatch Institute, 2004.
Willie Soon	*Global Warming: A Guide to the Science.* Vancouver, BC: Fraser Institute, Center for Studies in Risk and Regulation, 2001.
James Gustave Speth	*Red Sky at Morning: America and the Crisis of the Global Environment.* New Haven, CT: Yale University Press, 2005.
Michael Tenneson	*The Complete Idiot's Guide to Global Warming.* Indianapolis: Alpha, 2004.
Vijay V. Vaitheeswaran	*Power to the People: How the Coming Energy Revolution Will Transform an Industry, Change Our Lives, and Maybe Even Save the Planet.* New York: Farrar, Straus & Giroux, 2003.
David G. Victor	*The Collapse of the Kyoto Protocol and the Struggle to Slow Global Warming.* Princeton, NJ: Princeton University Press, 2001.
Spencer R. Weart	*The Discovery of Global Warming.* Cambridge, MA: Harvard University Press, 2003.

Index